Old & New
QUILT PATTERNS
in the Southern Tradition

Old & New
QUILT PATTERNS
IN THE SOUTHERN TRADITION

✛

Bets Ramsey

Rutledge Hill Press
Nashville, Tennessee

Photographs provided by The Quilts of Tennessee Study Project and published with permission.

Tennessee Heritage Quilt by permission of the Thursday Bee of the Smoky Mountain Quilters, Knoxville, Tennessee.

Drawings by the author.

Design: Harriette Bateman
Typography: Bailey Typography

Published in Nashville, Tennessee, by Rutledge Hill Press, 513 Third Avenue South, Nashville, Tennessee 37210

Library of Congress Cataloging-in-Publication Data

Ramsey, Bets, 1923-
    Old & new quilt patterns in the southern tradition / Bets Ramsey.
        p.   cm.
    Bibliography: p. 112
    Includes index.
    ISBN 0-934395-63-2
    1. Quilting—Patterns.   I. Title.   II. Title: Old and new quilt patterns in the southern tradition. III. Title: Quilt patterns.
TT835.R34   1987
746.9'7'0975—dc19   87-25182
                                                          CIP
        2   3   4   5   6   7   8   —   92   91   90   89   88
        Manufactured in the United States of America

CONTENTS

❖

PREFACE

❖

My fascination with fabric began at an early age with the making of doll clothes, and by thirteen I was making all my own garments. As an adult I became an exhibiting fiber artist in fabric collage, embroidery, and other forms of surface design, eventually quilting.

My study of southern quilts began in 1971 when I discovered a group of family quilts made in Redbud, Georgia, in the nineteenth century. Two aunts, Ollie McBrayer and Vinnye Carroll, and my father, Lee Miller, born in the 1880s, were able to give me personal recollections of quiltmaking and related activities that took place on their cotton-producing farm. Their stories and the quilts they had brought from Redbud gave me a link to a grandmother I had never known, Elizabeth Borders Miller.

Soon after, Harold and Ellen Lewis Buell Cash invited me to come to Wildwood, Georgia, to see the collection of quilts inherited from their relatives in Georgia, Tennessee, and Ohio. It was there I first saw a stuffed quilt from Rhea County, Tennessee. I have examined many more since then. T. Fred Miller, a Chattanooga photographer, accompanied me, as he did on numerous occasions, to photograph the quilts.

I made additional surveys of other significant private collections. The Z. C. and Sarah Key Patten collection, in Georgia's Chattanooga Valley, includes numerous North Carolina quilts. Leila Wert, from the same area, gathered quilts from many southern states. In the eastern corner of Tennessee, Virginia Caldwell, of Blountville, showed me quilts made in South Carolina, Virginia, North Carolina, and Tennessee. From these beginnings grew an increasing interest in quilt history and research.

Ten years after my introduction to quiltmaking, Ruth Holmberg, publisher of the *Chattanooga Times,* suggested I write a column on quilting. She was concerned, however, that I might not find enough material to sustain a weekly column. More often I have had to choose from an abundance of subjects. I am grateful for Mrs. Holmberg's encouragement and the opportunity to produce "The Quilter," now in its sixth year of publication. Wes Hasden offered sound advice during the column's formative period and continues to give support. I am indebted to the *Times* for permission to use much of the material included here.

Through the years my research has concentrated on quilts of the southeastern United States, particularly those states nearest Tennessee. The Kentucky Quilt Project's exhibition and book, *Kentucky Quilts 1800–1900,* made me realize that a similar effort needed to be undertaken in Tennessee. The proposal appealed to my friend Merikay Waldvogel, and we became co-directors of the Tennessee Quilt Study, sharing the investigative process, forming an exhibition, and writing a book, *The Quilts of Tennessee: Images of Domestic Life Prior to 1930.* I am grateful for her enthusiasm, her organizational skills, and, above all, her friendship. She directed the complicated process of photography for our quilt study and has kindly allowed certain reproductions for this book.

Requests for typical southern quilt patterns led me to gather material from "The Quilter" column, the Tennessee Quilt Study, and my own research for inclusion in this book. None of this could have been done without the willing sharing of many quilt owners who graciously allowed interviews and photographs. They have my abundant thanks.

My task was made easier by the never-failing encouragement of my husband, Paul Ramsey, and the editorial assistance of my daughter, Sarah Farmer. Their many kindnesses are appreciated.

Bets Ramsey
July 19, 1987

INTRODUCTION

❖

Nearly everyone likes quilts. As reminders of home, childhood, aunts, grandmothers, and others who gave affection, they stir memories in all of us. Quilts offer warmth and protection. They give comfort and security. They retain something of the maker's spirit, and they reward us with beauty of color and design.

Quilts are a significant part of American history, yet they seldom reach the textbooks. They record women's work as it was practiced in the setting of family life. In addition to providing evidence of home industry, quilts give clues to social customs, trade and commerce—even political action. As objects of design and craftsmanship, they have been included in art history, as well. Quilting and appliqué have been practiced for many hundreds of years, and examples are found in cultures throughout the world. Innovative quiltmakers of this country have developed geometric pieced work to a fine art.

Southern women have earned a deserved reputation for quality and ingenuity in quiltmaking. In times when women were limited in their outlets, making quilts was an acceptable means of personal and creative expression. Its forms have ranged from the earliest appliqué and whole-cloth quilts of the coastal states, the intricate quilting and stuffing in the mid-1800s, the strong, bold pieced work of the late nineteenth century, through delightful scrap quilts to the most modern of quilts and wall hangings.

Southern quiltmakers have been especially productive during certain decades of the nineteenth and twentieth centuries. Many fine appliqué quilts were made between 1825 and 1860, along with practical everyday quilts, when growing cotton was a way of life. Between 1880 and 1900, after the post-Civil War interval, another period of quiltmaking activity occurred owing to the increased production of cotton fabric that made inexpensive cloth readily available.

On a national level, the revival of colonial architecture and interior design in the 1920s fostered a return to handcrafted furnishings and quiltmaking. During the Great Depression of the 1930s, housewives made quilts for economy's sake. The craft movement of the 1960s, interest generated by *Roots* in the seventies, and the Bicentennial celebration, sparked an international renaissance that continues to this writing.

Style, fashion, and economics have often dictated the course of quiltmaking, and fads have come and gone, sometimes to return again. Not everyone chooses to stay in the shifting mainstream. Even when quiltmaking had lost its popularity in other parts of the country, many capable women in the South, not affected by outside influences, continued to make quilts—out of habit, necessity, pride, and desire. They found pleasure in their work.

I have seen a broad spectrum of southern quilts in my sixteen years of research and can confirm a long tradition of fine quiltmaking. This book pays tribute to all those who contributed to the making of that tradition as well as to those who will preserve and continue it.

TERMS AND NOTES

Appliqué: pieces of cloth laid on and sewn to a background material.

Backing: material used as the underside of the quilt.

Batt: a small unit of cotton or wool filler combed by hand with wire brushes called cards. Also factory-made in a single sheet.

Batting: the padding or filler of a quilt.

Binding: finish for the raw edge of the quilt, done with a strip of straight or bias material.

Block: unit or section of a quilt made of joined pieces or pieces applied to background material.

Border: solid, pieced, or appliquéd band at outer edge of quilt or surrounding center medallion.

Combination: block using both piecing and appliqué.

Design: the overall organization of a quilt, or a specific pattern.

Filler: batting, the padding of a quilt, usually wool or cotton, placed between the top and bottom fabric of the quilt.

Frame (or quilting frame): basically four strips of wood in rectangular position to which the quilt's three layers are fastened prior to quilting.

Grain of the material (or straight-of-the-goods): lengthwise and crosswise threads of the material used as guides in the placement of cutting-patterns.

Lining: material used on the underside of the quilt.

Master pattern: pattern which is reserved and from which working patterns are cut.

Pattern: the design of a quilt, most designs being traditional; also, the unit used to cut out pieces for quiltmaking.

Patchwork: pieces of fabric seamed together, as in pieced work, or applied to a background, as in appliqué, and joined together to make a whole.

Pieced work: pieces joined by seaming together to make a whole, usually in geometric design.

Quilt: two layers of cloth stitched or tied together with padding between.

Quilter's knot: a single knot made by passing the needle through a loop of thread.

Quilting: stitching through layers of fabric and padding.

Sashing (or stripping): band added between blocks in joining.

Selvage: edge of cloth where weft thread turns back.

Set: the fabric used between blocks in joining or the arrangement in which blocks are joined. *To set:* to put the blocks together.

String piecing: the joining of narrow strips of fabric, usually in random size, to make a unit.

Stuffed work: the addition of extra filler to quilted or appliquéd designs to make a raised surface.

Top: the upper and outer layer of a quilt.

Warp: the threads running lengthwise in a loom when weaving cloth.

Weft: the yarn carried across the warp when weaving cloth.

Wholecloth: quilt top of solid material without appliqué or piecing, often three panels seamed together, quilted, and sometimes stuffed.

Notes:

No seam allowance has been included on pattern pieces. Add three-sixteenths or one-quarter inch to all sides of each pattern piece.

When a block size is given, it is the size of the finished block. While in progress the block will be larger to include seam allowance.

Old & New
QUILT PATTERNS
in the Southern Tradition

THE MAKING OF A QUILT

The Quilt Defined

A quilt has three layers. The upper layer, or *quilt top*, may be made from one piece of material or several pieces seamed together to make one piece, a *wholecloth quilt*. A second type of top is constructed from many small pieces joined together into a *pieced top*. A third type, *appliqué*, is made by sewing, or applying, cut-out pieces of cloth onto a background fabric. Piecing and appliqué may be combined to make a *combination quilt*.

The middle of a quilt is called the *filler, batting*, or *stuffing*. Today polyester batting is the most popular filler because it is easy to sew through, is light-weight yet warm, and launders well. Before the advent of synthetic batting, cotton was the primary filler used in the South. Sometimes the cotton was homegrown, ginned, and then carded into small rectangles that were stacked up until they were needed for a quilt. More often, it was a purchased cotton batt. In rural areas where cotton was not raised, quilters sometimes used wool or feathers for filler. When a quilt became worn, the frugal housewife covered it with a new top and back, added some stitches, and gave the quilt a longer life. Worn blankets and even grass, leaves, newspaper, burlap, or rags have been discovered in old quilts.

A *quilt back* or *lining* provides the bottom of the quilt. Bleached or unbleached muslin, percale, prints, flour sacks, and handwoven materials have all been used for backing, because they are not difficult to sew through yet are sturdy enough to withstand wear. Most sheets are too closely woven to be suitable. A quilt back should be compatible with its top in simplicity or elegance as well as color.

The three layers are joined by stitches that go through all thicknesses, from top to bottom and back, again and again—the *quilting*.

Getting A Good Start

Many readers with a firm knowledge of quilting will find this section a review that offers several new ideas. Less experienced quilters and beginners should be able to follow these basic lessons to fulfilling conclusions. Four of the terms you will see most often appear below. (See "Terms and Notes" on page *x* for more quilting vocabulary.)

Block: unit usually made of several pieces joined together.

Grain of the material or *straight-of-the-goods:* line parallel to the length (warp) of the cloth or at right angles to it (weft).

Patchwork: surface made by seaming smaller pieces together to make a whole (pieced) or pieces sewn on top of a background piece (appliqué).

Selvage: edge made on cloth when weft thread turns back.

My own rules for quiltmaking are simple.
1. Wash the material; iron when dry.
2. Remove the selvages.
3. Be conscious of the grain of the fabric. Ideally, when pieces are sewn together, all the threads will run vertically and horizontally, as in a sheet.
4. Use good, sharp scissors.
5. Check your accuracy in drafting and cutting.
6. Employ careful workmanship.

If you are a beginner, start with an easy pattern like the Nine Patch, Pinwheel, or Roman Stripe. Plan to make one block as a sample. If the pattern works out well, you may wish to proceed with a quilt, but often a pillow top will satisfy the beginner.

Selecting the Pattern

The Nine Patch block, an enduring favorite with quilters, is a good beginning. A pattern preschoolers learn at their grandmothers' knees and that grandmothers can follow when their eyes grow dim, the Nine Patch can be plain or fancy. Make a homey version using sewing scraps that suggest pleasant family memories. If you want elegance, that's possible, too. A Washington decorator once made a Nine Patch of silk and velvet swatches from fabrics used in the White House in 1904.

The block's nine equally-sized squares do not imply dullness. Innumerable possibilities for manipulating color and joining blocks account for the design's popularity. Nine is a satisfying number to work with, as is three. Try it and see.

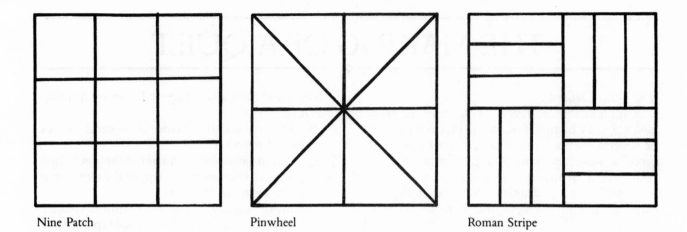

Nine Patch   Pinwheel   Roman Stripe

Making the Pattern

Begin by drawing a square of any size; a four-inch square is easy to work with, but it can be larger or smaller. Almost any kind of paper that will not crumble or tear easily—some junk mail is ideal—can serve your pattern-making purpose. To insure accuracy, you may choose to draw the pattern on graph paper. Test the square by folding it diagonally after cutting it to see if the corners match. If they don't, try making another square. This square, then, is the size of the finished piece. To make a cutting pattern, add a ¼ or 3/16-inch seam allowance to all sides of the square. Some quilters prefer to use a 3/16-inch allowance if the material is firm and does not ravel. Cut on or to the inner edge of the pencil line to avoid increasing the size of your square.

Once the pattern is made, you may duplicate it on a heavier piece of paper, cardboard, sandpaper, or plastic. Keep the first as your *Master Pattern* in case you need a duplicate later. Pattern edges do get worn after much use.

Patterns in this book may be traced on an overlying sheet of thin paper. *Add desired seam allowance to all sides.* Mark the master pattern and make several cutting patterns to use.

Selecting the Fabric

Choose cloth that really appeals to you; then your block will speak for you. You may want two, three, even nine different pieces of material to use in making the Nine Patch block.

Most quilters prefer 100 percent cotton—neither too thin nor too heavy—or a cotton-polyester blend. It should be washed and ironed when you buy it so it will be ready when you need it. Washing removes sizing and odors and prevents later shrinkage.

Cutting the Patches

Pin your pattern onto the cloth or draw around it with a #3 thin-lead pencil. Do not use a ball-point pen, for the ink might run in future washing. Some quilters doubt the safety of "disappearing" pencils which may contain harmful chemicals.

Remove selvages; place the pattern with the grain of the material, and cut out nine squares. Use sharp scissors that make a clean edge. Try placing the pieces in different positions until you have found the way you like best. By laying the pieces out in a block, you will know where you are going as you join them together, either by hand or machine.

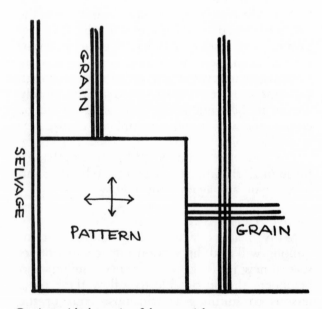

Cutting with the grain of the material

Nine squares of cloth can be put together in many arrangements. These illustrations may help you discover combinations for prints and solids. Each plan seems to make a new design out of the familiar Nine Patch. Other ideas will occur as you experiment; so jot them down for future development. Possibilities for the Nine Patch have never been exhausted!

Nine Patch variations

Joining the Pieces

To join the pieces by hand, use the needle which works best for you. I prefer a #8 or #10 crewel needle for hand sewing with a single #50 sewing thread of cotton or cotton and polyester. Many quilters start and stop their sewing with two or three backstitches. If you prefer, a single knot may be made by passing the needle through a loop of thread. A single backstitch holds the knot in place. A fat, rolled knot is not acceptable.

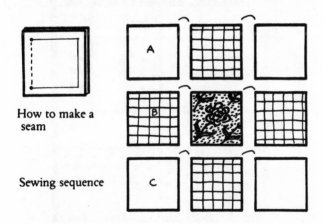

How to make a seam

Sewing sequence

Sew your first two squares together beginning at the inner edge of the seam allowance, from dot to dot as shown. With your fingers or a dry iron, press the seams to one side for greater strength. Piecing may be done by machine in the same way, starting and stopping with a few backstitches.

After joining the squares in row A, do the next two rows across. Then join row A, the top row, to row B, the center row, and finally row C to row B, carefully matching the seams and corners exactly. The design's total impact will be lost if the pieces are mismatched.

Press the seams of the completed Nine Patch to one side, preferably the light fabric going toward the dark. Be sure seams are straight and unit corners meet properly. Measure to see if the block is the correct size. If four-inch squares were used, the block should be twelve inches plus seam allowance.

Bordering the Block

Next add a one-and-a-half or two-inch border to frame your block. Use one of the fabrics already in the block or something that harmonizes well. Choose another fabric for a corner square the same width as the border. Press seams to one side. Check to be sure corners are square, not splayed out, adjusting seams as necessary until they are square.

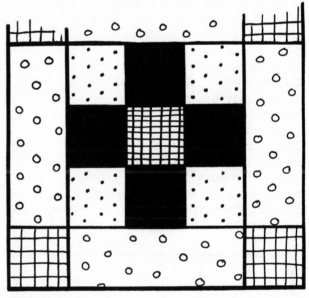

Bordered Nine Patch

Use your Nine Patch block for a cushion top, a pot holder, the panel on a tote bag, or the first block of a quilt. Although you may like your square just the way it is, the addition of batting and quilting will make it even more splendid.

Preparing to Quilt

To complete the quilting process, you will need a backing about an inch wider (for safety's sake) than the size of the top. It may be a matching or contrasting material or simple cotton muslin. Select a fairly thin batting, bonded or needle-locked. Cut it to the size of the back. Pin the top, batting, and backing together; baste diagonally in two directions across the square and then around the outer edges.

Quilting the Block

You may want to put the basted block in a small hoop or frame for quilting, but it is not absolutely necessary for a small practice piece. For your first pieces, use quilting thread that matches the fabric. When you are a better quilter, you may want to use contrasting thread for emphasis.

Several kinds of quilting thread are available. Your thread should be compatible with the cloth and not so strong that it will eventually wear through the material. The usual quilting threads are stronger than sewing thread. They make the filler stand up around the stitches because they do not stretch like polyester thread. Most quilting thread is already coated to prevent snarling, but you may wish to use beeswax to smooth it even more. Soft quilting—not in a frame—can be done with a sewing needle (again I use a #8-crewel needle), but if the piece is put in a frame, use a quilting needle called a *between*. A #8, #9, or #10 may feel right to you—the larger the number, the smaller the needle.

For the Nine Patch, you may want to do a design that contrasts with the basic shapes of the patches to give your composition a counterpoint. Use masking tape ¼-inch wide or fine pencil lines made with a #3 mechanical pencil as a guidemarker. Dark fabric requires a white colored pencil or a sliver of soap for marking.

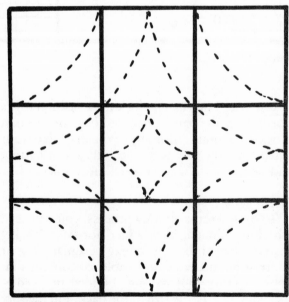

Contrast in quilting

Make a single knot, pull it through from the top, leaving the tail between the batting and the top. Take a backstitch to secure the knot; then sew the running stitch as evenly and rhythmically as you can, going all the way through the three layers. Start from the center of the block and work outward. To end the stitches, backstitch in a seam or, if you are doing a pillow top, on the underside (which will be within). You will find further quilting tips in a later section of this book, "The Quilting of a Quilt" (page 26).

Finishing the Block

When your quilting is finished, complete the block appropriately for its intended use. If your square is to be a pillow top, cut a matching or similar piece of material and seam the two pieces together, leaving an opening in what is now the outer pillowcase. Make a separate case to stuff and enclose. Blind-stitch each opening shut.

Your block may be incorporated into a tote bag or an apron bib. For a table hot pad, bind the edge with matching or contrasting binding. Add a loop or ring to the corner for a pot holder.

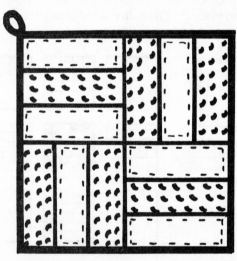

Roman Stripe potholder

Basics for Good Quiltmaking

The steps described above, plus a few more, apply to making a quilt. Before starting out, however, select a pattern and make a few trial blocks in different fabrics to gain some idea of color possibilities and to see if you enjoy working a particular pattern. If you are not pleased with the results, try another pattern.

After you have chosen a design, begin gathering material. Do you wish to limit the number of colors used for an orderly effect, or do you like the random, scrap-bag look? If you plan to buy material, calculate how much you will need by laying out one block, color by color, measuring the amount required and multiplying by the number of blocks in your plan. A two-color quilt for a double bed will require about four yards of each color plus another two or more yards for bordering.

Lay the block on the bed and measure to see how many blocks it will take to cover the top of the bed; then add enough for the side and bottom overhangs, and a pillow-tuck, if needed. You will then know what lies ahead of you. By now, you realize you are making a heavy commitment of time; quiltmaking cannot be enjoyed if you watch the clock.

After you have selected your material, wash and iron it and remove the selvages. Make patterns of the unit pieces you will need. Place your pieces on the fabric so the grain of the material will be continuous when the units are sewn together. This will insure a squared-up top.

Use good, sharp scissors or a rotary cutter; there is no substitute. Accuracy in cutting is of utmost importance for good results.

Plan your cutting in an efficient manner. You may be able to lay off some pieces with a pencil and ruler or yardstick instead of cutting single units. Well-organized work moves more quickly than ill-prepared work. Place the cut pieces in neat stacks in a flat box for easy reach and orderliness. This is essential for effective work on the sewing machine.

Be sure corners match and triangle points are not taken up in seams. Stripped blocks must be lined up accurately. Corners should be square and not splayed out. Check size of seams and size of blocks as you go along to insure uniformity.

As you work, be thinking of methods to improve your assembly. All quiltmakers find their own tricks and establish their own discipline. Ask yourself if there is a better way; then try it. Your individuality speaks through your work.

Check this list to see how you measure up.

A Guide for Good Quiltmaking
 1. Wash and iron material to remove sizing and allow for shrinkage.
 2. Use accurate patterns of durable material.
 3. Draw around the pattern on the fabric with pencil, careful to keep the exact shape.
 4. Cut one piece at a time on the line with sharp scissors or rotary cutter.
 5. Do not use the selvage.
 6. Place patterns on the grain of the material so the finished block's grain is uniform throughout.
 7. Take seam allowance exactly to measure.
 8. Check size of units with tape measure or ruler to insure accuracy before joining to make block and then before joining blocks.
 9. Make smooth, even stitches with matching single thread using small quilter's knot and finishing with three backstitches.
10. Match corners and points of joining exactly.
11. Press seams to one side, the dark side, if relevant.
12. Choose fabrics, preferably cotton, which have pleasing pattern, not too busy or spotty.
13. Combine colors which both contrast and harmonize (See "Color for Quilters" section).
14. Try the same pattern in sample blocks using different colors and fabrics to explore possibilities.

ALL ABOUT PATTERNS

How to Make a Simple Pattern:
YELLOW POPLAR LEAF

Everybody loves the first crisp leaves of fall. Steps quicken and housework seems lighter; we tackle even unpleasant chores with enthusiasm.

Pick up some leaves and study them for quiltmaking possibilities. Through the years leaves have inspired many patterns for quilters. You may want to use one of the old standards for a quilt, but it is easy to do an original design by employing a real leaf for the pattern.

Almost any leaf can be used for an appliqué design. Draw around a single leaf or use a group of leaves to make a pattern. A single leaf can be used in a repeated sequence; its natural lines provide a fine outline with hardly any work at all.

The illustrated leaf is a pieced design—easy to draw if you follow the simple rules of pattern drafting. This leaf has been shown in many pattern books through the years under the name of Autumn Leaf, Maple Leaf, Magnolia Leaf, and Tea Leaf. I like to think of it as the tulip tree or yellow poplar. You will notice a close relationship to the popular Bear Paw.

Take a piece of paper eight to ten inches square (or a size of your choice); fold it in thirds in both directions to make nine equal sections. Divide the

sections according to the illustration. You will see that only two pattern pieces are required: a square and a triangle, plus a strip for a stem. Add seam allowance all the way around each piece to complete your patterns.

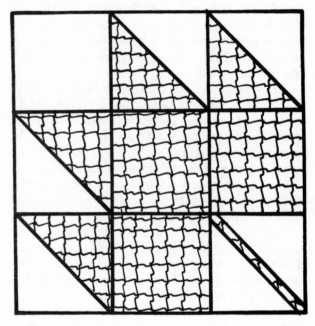

Yellow Poplar Leaf pattern

The search for colors will be the next step in planning your quilt. You may make your leaves from the same fabric throughout or use scrap pieces to give the feeling of many-colored autumn leaves. After completing a number of blocks, think about joining them. Try laying four blocks together to make a larger block or placing your blocks in rows with leaves going in the same direction, stripped or not. Leaves can also be placed in various directions, just as real leaves fall from trees. Alternate plain with pieced blocks or arrange them randomly. Your quilt will be colorful however you assemble the squares.

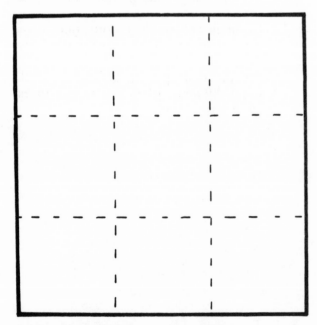

Square of paper folded into nine sections

Another Pattern Exercise: SAILING SHIP

"There is nothing—absolutely nothing—half so much worth doing as simply messing about in boats," said Water Rat in *The Wind in the Willows.* Many Southerners agree, and quilters certainly enjoy nautical ideas, because quilting manuals offer many: The Ship, Fishing Boats, Tall Ships, The Mayflower, Sailboat, Dutch Boat, Ocean Waves, Storm at Sea, Mariner's Compass, and Anchor. In addition to these pieced patterns, there have been splendid nautical appliqué designs made, especially in the nineteenth century when New England ships went around the world.

The Ship is an easy pattern to draw for yourself. Decide what size you want the finished block. Cut a piece of paper that size. Divide it

The completed ship

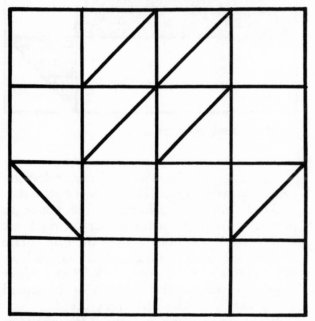

Layout for ship

into four equal sections in each direction by folding or drawing lines to make sixteen squares. Fill in the design as illustrated. To simplify your work, erase any unnecessary lines so as to make fewer small units. Add seam allowance around all pieces.

Plan colors and fabric which evoke a nautical feeling. Think of the water you know. It may be blue or green, muddy brown like the Mississippi, or even black like swamp water. Skies are blue sometimes but pink at sunset, red in the morning ("Red sky at night, sailor's delight/Red sky at morning, sailors take warning!") or white with fog. Sails are white or orange, red, yellow, blue, or green. Your sailing ship will show what experiences you have had and where you have been.

For variation, make ship blocks to border a quilt in the Ocean Waves pattern or appliqué a large center panel depicting a favorite beach house or lighthouse with ships sailing around the panel. Ship blocks may be alternated with plain blocks in which you quilt anchors or life preservers. Your ship blocks may be quilted with waves in the water and clouds in the sky. Many possibilities exist in developing this design if you let your imagination drift or sail away. Bon voyage!

Drafting a Pattern: Basket of Scraps

Quiltmakers really enjoy basket-pattern quilts, whose variations date back at least 150 years. Barbara Brackman shows seventy in her *Encyclopedia of Pieced Quilt Patterns*.

About 1880, the Blair sisters of Roane County, Tennessee, made the "flowers and leaves" in their basket of assorted dressmaking scraps in shades of brown and tan. The lower portion of the basket, made with no base, used unbleached muslin, and the blocks were set together with a square of brown-dotted fabric. They set each block on the diagonal so their baskets would stand upright when the quilt was placed on the bed.

Nearly a hundred years later, Dr. Roy Ward of Watkinsville, Georgia, chose the same pattern for a wall hanging to go in a friend's office, but he did not try to make his quilt look like an antique. He chose contemporary colors and fabric, using shades of red, purple, and off-white, mixing them up like a true Basket of Scraps. He placed a square of print material between each pieced block as the Blair sisters had done. Follow these directions to echo his efforts.

For a ten-inch block, draw a square 10″ x 10″ with a well-sharpened pencil, a ruler with a truly

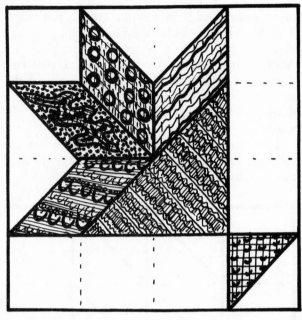

Dr. Ward's Basket of Scraps

straight edge, and brown, gift wrap or drawing paper. Mark each side of the square at two-and-a-half-inch intervals, connecting the points to make a grid of four squares by four squares. Look at the design and draw it onto the grid. Erase unneeded sections of the grid and you will have the diagram of the pieced block. If you prefer larger or smaller blocks, simply draw the desired size, divide it into fourths, and proceed.

Next trace each unit on tissue or tracing paper; **add a seam allowance** to all sides of each unit. There are six units to this block: one large triangle, two medium triangles, two small triangles, two rectangles, one square, four diamonds. Transfer the tissue paper pattern to a stronger, firmer pattern material, taking care to be accurate. (Note: If you should copy patterns on a copy machine, be aware that the size may be slightly altered.)

Once you learn to dissect quilt patterns, almost any pattern can be yours.

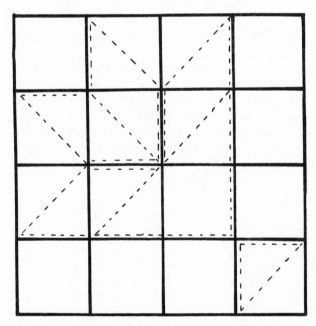

Pattern layout

One More Drafting Lesson: BEA'S BASKET

One day a friend of mine, Beatrice Birdsong, showed me a family quilt she wanted to copy. Her mother-in-law, Minnie Ordway Birdsong of Nashville, Tennessee, an enthusiastic quilter, had made it for Bea about 1935. Bea had cherished it and used it sparingly out of respect for its maker.

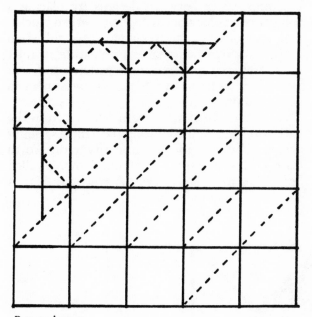

Pattern layout

Her quilt utilized the familiar Basket-of-Scraps pattern but each block was larger, each basket distinguishable by a handle made of three appliquéd triangles set somewhat askew. None of the seventy basket patterns in quilt encyclopedias sported a handle like Bea's so we set to work drafting a pattern.

Bea chose blue-gray for the background material, a print of rust, orange, green, and brown for the basket. We laid out the design on a 15 x 15-inch square divided at 3-inch intervals, traced each piece on tissue paper, added the seam allowance, and cut work patterns from a heavier paper. Each basket involved thirty-three pieces instead of the more usual twelve and thus needed more work to insure a proper fit. Block assembly was similar to the Basket of Scraps but required more time since the blocks were larger; however, Bea used fewer to complete her quilt top.

Bea's Basket is useful in underscoring another lesson. When preparing to draft a pattern, first look for a basic division. In this case it was a grid of five squares by five squares. Draw the desired size of the finished block and divide it into twenty-five squares. If a 15-inch block seems too large, try a 12½-inch block marked off into 2½-inch squares in both directions. Draw the accompanying design onto your grid, erasing unnecessary lines. For the handle, divide the two outer rows in half. Your completed drawing will be the exact size of a completed block. Proceed with tracing, adding seam allowance, and making a cutting pattern.

When using a pattern with numerous pieces, make a trial block before continuing in order to test your accuracy. If the seam allowance is the least bit off, your pieces will not fit together properly; results will be lamentable.

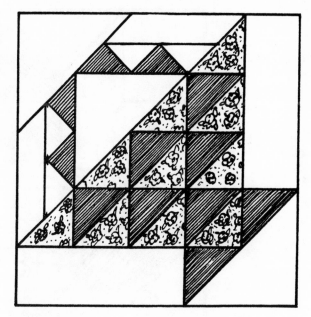

Bea's Basket

Arrowhead Star: *Tennessee Honeysuckle*

✤

One of the best ways to plunge into quiltmaking when you are a novice is to make a sampler quilt. When I worked with Senior Neighbors quilt groups, we did a series of forty-two sampler blocks to build confidence and proficiency, to increase familiarity with a variety of patterns, and to allow for good experiences in color manipulation. Some of the resulting quilts were color-coordinated; others were scrap quilts with a bold array of colors.

Once their blocks were finished, my students had to figure out the best way to join their handiwork. Some quilters chose to set block to block for a happy interplay from pattern to pattern. Some used stripping between the blocks. Light-hued stripping brought out the bright colors in blocks. Figured stripping made a pleasant blending of fabrics. A few provided a breathing space between designs by placing a solid or print block between their worked blocks.

If you don't want to undertake a full-sized quilt, try a wall hanging or a miniature sampler quilt. You can experiment with patterns or invent your own without a tremendous investment in time or money.

As a start, here is a pattern selected from the 1,425 quilts examined during the Tennessee quilt project. You may notice a similarity to the North Carolina Lily pattern, but this quilt's owner called hers *Tennessee Honeysuckle*. Arrowhead Star is another apt name for it.

ARROWHEAD STAR
Maker: Judy Lee Winfree Barnett
Smith County, Tennessee, c. 1880
Assorted scraps set with blue sashing and white squares.

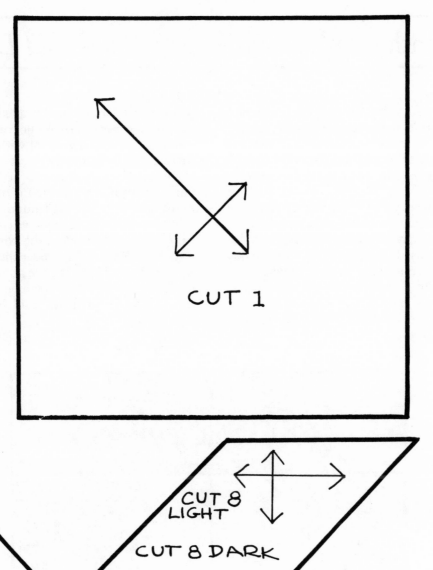

CUT 1

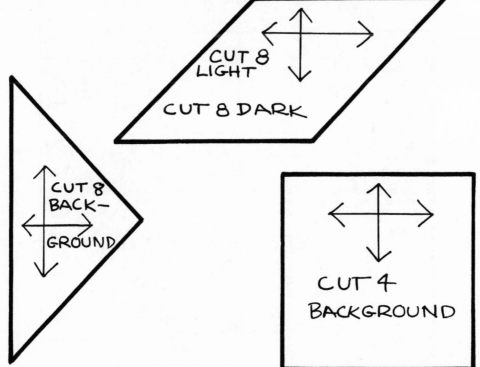

CUT 8
LIGHT

CUT 8 DARK

CUT 8
BACK-
GROUND

CUT 4
BACKGROUND

Arrowhead Star
10-inch block
Add seam allowance to all sides of patterns. The pattern is
related to Turkey Tracks on page 102.

Gentleman's Bowtie: *The Good Old Days*

The Gentleman's Bowtie pattern is one of those old favorites that's been around as long as your grandmother can remember. It uses up various scraps and is easy to assemble. Seeing such a quilt evokes a lot of memories that people like to share.

Set up a quilt frame at a craft fair or shopping mall and watch people gather. Talk will be about the good old days "when my mother [or grandmother] used to quilt." Quilters enjoy hearing these recollections; it gives them a sense of belonging to a long chain of quiltmakers reaching far back in time and continuing into the future. Some of my friends at the Mary Walker Towers in Chattanooga recalled the years when they were growing up. While country life meant a lot of hard work, it was not without pleasure and there always was plenty to eat.

"We had quilt frames attached to the ceiling so you could pull the frame up out of the way at night when you weren't quilting. Quilting was winter work because there was too much to do in summer. I liked to card the cotton and make it into batts. We'd lay up under the quilt and thread the needles and keep the fire going. You could see the high-top shoes the women were wearing. I was six or seven then," said James Cohill, an Alabamian.

GENTLEMAN'S BOWTIE
  Maker: Jemima Lamon
  Sevier County, Tennessee, c. 1915
  Assorted cotton scraps, four squares stripped together with rose or other colors; pieced blocks set alternately with red squares. (Quilt appears in color section.)

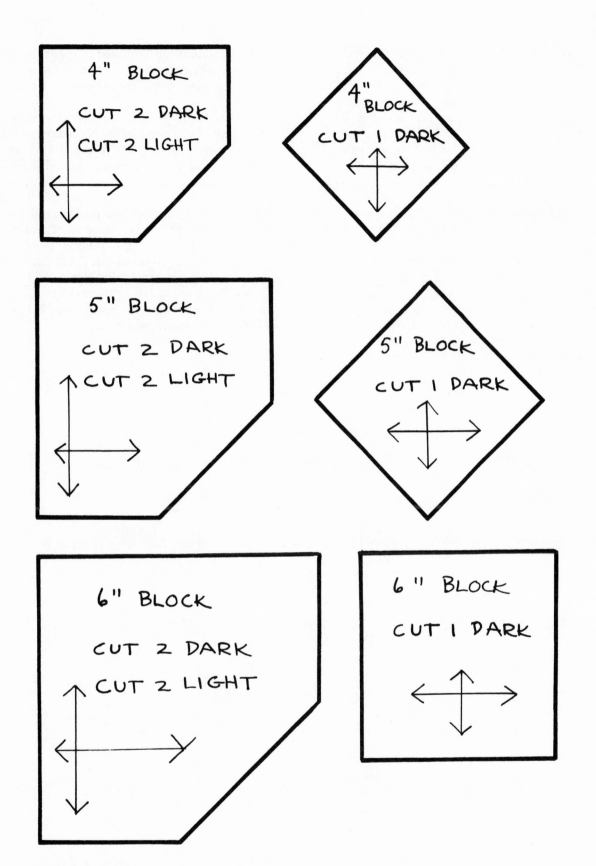

4" BLOCK

CUT 2 DARK

CUT 2 LIGHT

4" BLOCK

CUT 1 DARK

5" BLOCK

CUT 2 DARK

CUT 2 LIGHT

5" BLOCK

CUT 1 DARK

6" BLOCK

CUT 2 DARK

CUT 2 LIGHT

6" BLOCK

CUT 1 DARK

Gentleman's Bowtie
The pattern is presented in three sizes. Choose the size you
prefer and add a seam allowance to all sides.

Johnny Daniels said his folks allowed the children to keep money they made picking cotton on Saturday. When Monday rolled around his mother would say, "Now I want you to pick just as fast today as you did on Saturday. When you hit at a boll, have your hand set to get it all. When you hit at it and miss half, you have to go back and you could be picking the next one." Later they would go back to get the nabs (the leftovers) for home use in making quilts.

Geneva Ware's mother ordered bundles of scraps from Sears, Roebuck and Company to supplement her sewing scraps. She said the girls made quilts for their hope chests and for their brothers. Geneva recalled the patterns they used: Snake Wobble, Ocean Waves, Step to the Lighthouse, Gentleman's Bowtie, Hog-pen, Tree of Paradise, Monkey Wrench, Lone Star, Grandmother's Fan, Dutch Doll, Tulip, and string quilts made on paper.

Belle Fernandis remembered the pegs that held the frame together, the ball cotton for quilting thread, and the bundles of scraps from the country store.

Ruthenia Smith grew up in the city where her mother pieced warm quilts for everyday use from used clothing. Piecing both top and bottom layers, she would use an outing flannel sheet for the filler, then tie the layers together with yarn. Mrs. Smith's best quilts were quilted "by the piece," following the outline of each individual unit. For other quilts she chose to elbow-quilt; placing her elbow—as the pivotal point of a compass—on the edge of the quilt and with pencil or chalk in her hand, she would draw quarter-circles to the left again and again.

Today's quilters have an easier time. I wonder what their memories will be.

Little Britches: *Patterns Evoke Memories*

If you grew up with quilts, there was probably one you especially liked to sleep under, one that felt right or had particular meaning for you. Emily Cox of Paris, Tennessee, has just such a favorite. Although her collection is considerable, she really cherishes a rather plain-looking Little Britches quilt, because it was made from scraps associated with people dear to her. When Emily was badly hurt in an accident, a friend visited her in the hospital to try to bring some comfort. Emily was barely able to talk and in great pain. "Bring me a quilt from home," she said. "It will make me feel better." The friend brought Little Britches. Emily is convinced the warmth of home and the love of the family contained in that quilt speeded her recovery. (A Little Britches quilt appears among the colored photographs in this book.)

The quilts you are making today are the treasures of tomorrow. Your elegant appliqué quilts may be works of art saved for "when company comes," but the everyday quilts often have the most sentimental attachment because they are the ones you live with. Make fine quilts, but include some simpler ones, too.

A quilt may be an inanimate assortment of fibers to some, but others know each quilt is imbued with the spirit of its maker.

LITTLE BRITCHES
  Makers: Susie Drucilla Greer Cope and Addie Lee Cope Butler
  Henry County, Tennessee, c. 1920
  Scraps from family sewing in pieced blocks set with red and green calico and solid light green cotton fabric.

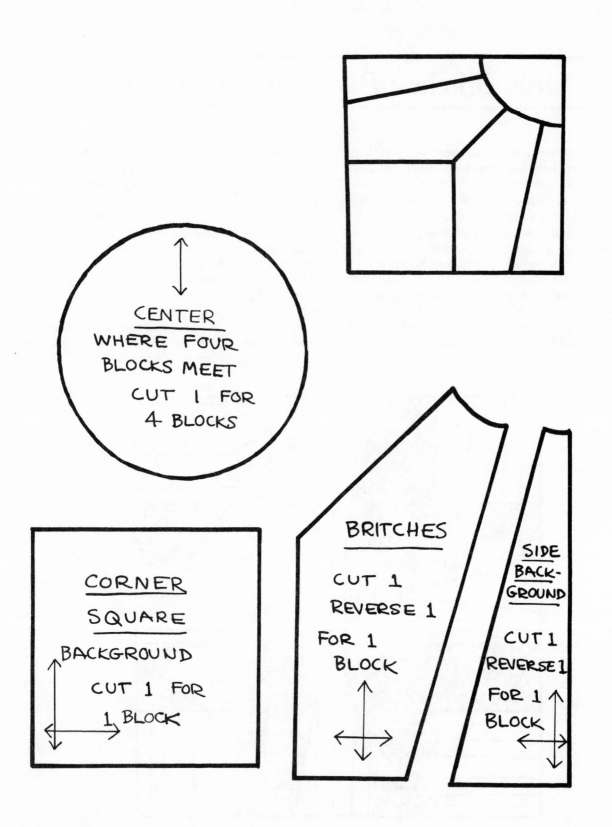

CENTER
WHERE FOUR
BLOCKS MEET
CUT 1 FOR
4 BLOCKS

CORNER
SQUARE
BACKGROUND
CUT 1 FOR
1 BLOCK

BRITCHES
CUT 1
REVERSE 1
FOR 1
BLOCK

SIDE
BACK-
GROUND
CUT 1
REVERSE 1
FOR 1
BLOCK

Little Britches
10-inch block
Side background piece is used when making four single
blocks, as illustrated, to join for the whole block. Place side
background piece on fold if you prefer to make the whole
block as shown on the preceding page.

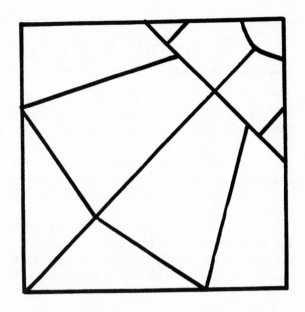

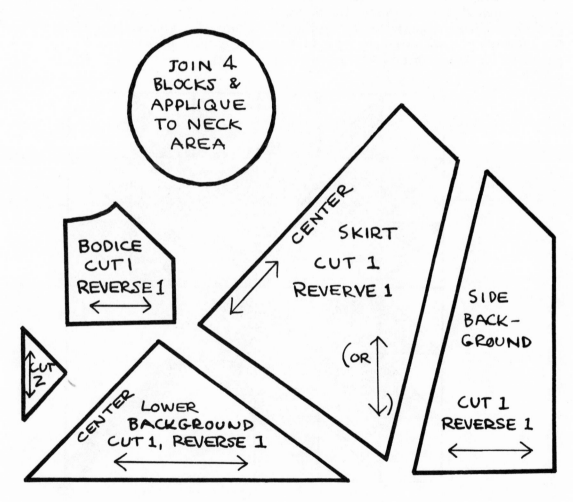

JOIN 4 BLOCKS & APPLIQUE TO NECK AREA

BODICE CUT 1 REVERSE 1

CENTER SKIRT CUT 1 REVERSE 1

(OR)

SIDE BACK-GROUND CUT 1 REVERSE 1

CUT 2

CENTER LOWER BACKGROUND CUT 1, REVERSE 1

Little Dresses
10-inch block
Perhaps little girls may prefer to have quilts with little dresses. Design by author.

Jonesborough Tree: *A Pattern from a Fair*

Quilt and patchwork patterns can be found in unexpected places. Jane McGehee of Johnson City, Tennessee, an alert viewer at an Old Jonesborough Days craft fair, found one she liked covering a vendor's table. She drew a sketch of it and in two days had made enough blocks for a small wall hanging.

The design is a small tree—just six-inches square. The pattern is like Bear Paw, with three pieced units set together at the inner corners, the "heels." A fourth block supplies a trunk for the tree.

Tree patterns make pleasing quilts and carry a sense of strength and continuity. The balanced proportion of Jane's tree attracted my attention; it was a friendly tree, not too tall, but straight. Jane put her six blocks together on the diagonal, with plain blocks in between, and surrounded it with a 4-inch border.

You can make the Jonesborough Tree to any scale by drawing your own pattern, or you can use one given here. The first will make a 6-inch block suitable for a child's quilt or wall hanging. The 10-inch block can be used for a large quilt.

The Jonesborough Tree lends itself to scrap-piecing or can be made from the same print throughout. I like each block made from a different material with the background the same for all blocks—not necessarily plain white or unbleached muslin. Try something different. This design is suitable for a group project, providing you can get everyone to take the same size seam allowance.

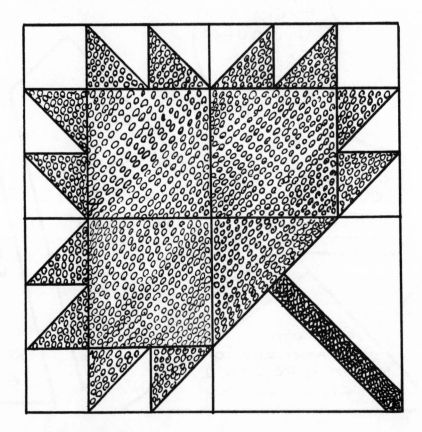

JONESBOROUGH TREE
Maker: Jane McGehee
Johnson City, Tennessee, 1983
Each block made of a different print alternates with a solid block on the diagonal.

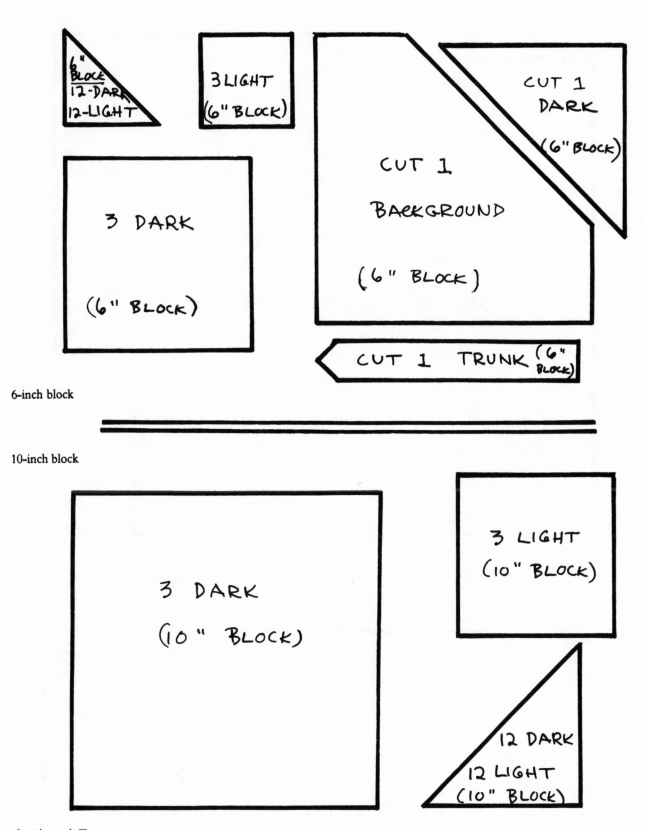

6-inch block

10-inch block

Jonesborough Tree
Use the patterns for the 6-inch block to make a small quilt or wall hanging. The 10-inch block is suitable for a full-sized bed quilt. One "Paw" section can be repeated in a Nine Patch to make the Bear Paw, another version of the same pattern.

Pattern continued on next page

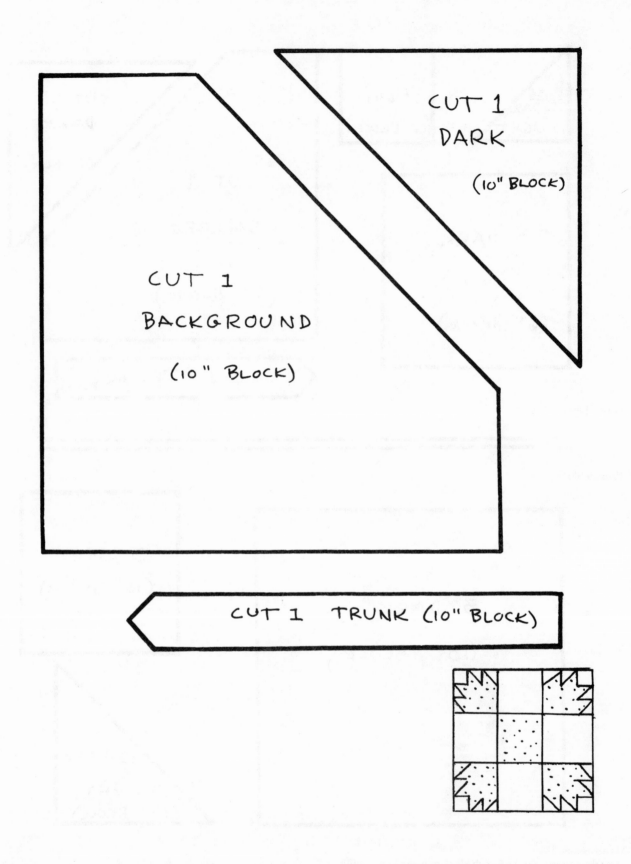

CUT 1
DARK

(10" BLOCK)

CUT 1

BACKGROUND

(10" BLOCK)

CUT 1   TRUNK (10" BLOCK)

Tennessee Tulip: *Creating a New Design*

Through the years quiltmakers have invented thousands of quilt patterns by altering old designs or dreaming up new ones. They frequently give regional or state names to their blocks: Road to California, Kansas Trouble, Texas Star, Ohio Rose, Virginia Reel, and North Carolina Lily. You may be able to invent a block that expresses an idea related to your locale. Talk over possibilities with your friends and family. Put a few sketches on paper to try out ideas. Make variations by rearranging the elements. When you have a pleasing design, draw it to the finished size, cut out the pattern pieces, add seam allowance, and make a sample block. Alter as necessary to improve the pattern. Then share your new design with other quiltmakers.

I devised a new Tennessee Tulip that can be made of scrap pieces or the same assortment of material throughout. The tulip, made of triangles, uses several shades of the same color; darker pieces in the lower part give depth. If you decide to make a quilt top, you may wish to have each flower in a different color. Leaves, too, can vary in material. Make a trial block to get acquainted with the pattern before you commit yourself to a big project.

The block is designed for a 12½-inch square, including the seam allowance for joining. I think the blocks look best set together without stripping since there is already some white space around the flowers. You may have other ideas of how to make your tulip garden.

The pattern is basically a four patch and can be assembled in four units before joining, or the tulip flower can be pieced, the side pieces added, and the top joined to the lower half.

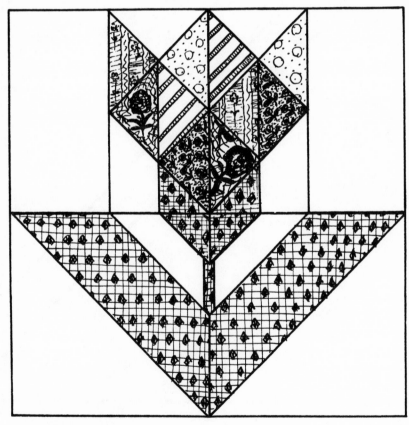

TENNESSEE TULIP
  Designer: the author
  Chattanooga, Tennessee, 1981
  Medley of colored scraps give depth to the flower.

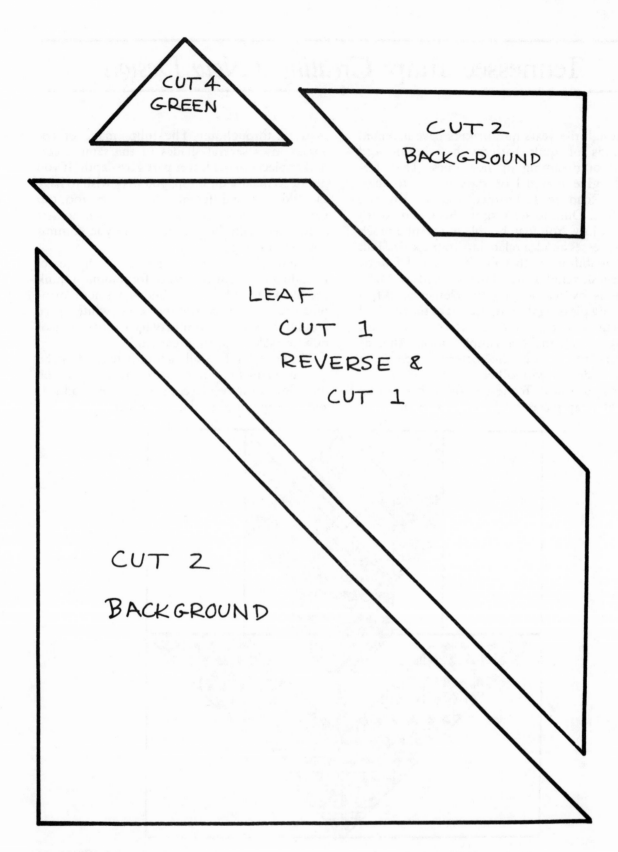

Tennessee Tulip
12-inch block
Tulips of different colors make a colorful quilt.

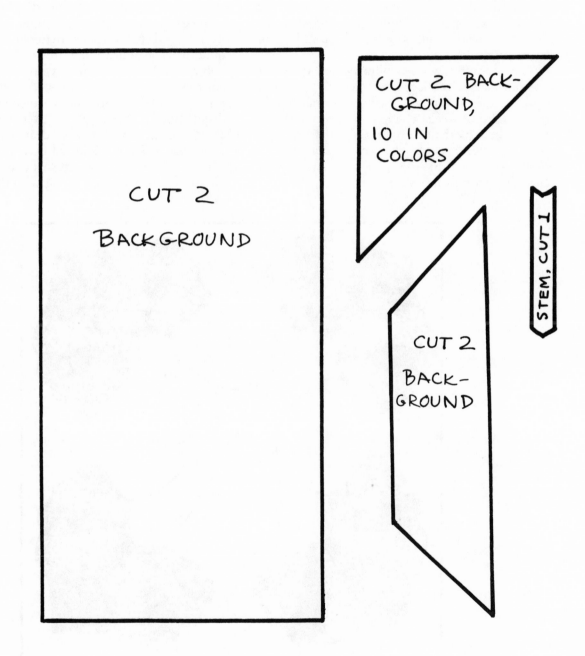

CUT 2

BACKGROUND

CUT 2 BACK-
GROUND,
10 IN
COLORS

STEM, CUT 1

CUT 2

BACK-
GROUND

Rocky Mountain Honeysuckle:
A Combination Pattern

During the survey of Tennessee quilts, my co-author and I had the help of wonderful volunteers who faithfully followed us on our rounds. We saw an assortment of quilts that included the finest of brides' quilts and the humblest of everyday quilts.

The men and women who helped us—two doctors, several college professors, a mayor, a strawberry grower, an engineer, some artists, farmers, housewives, children, and secretaries—found the experience exciting. The stories and family histories told by the quilt owners offered small windows to the past and heightened appreciation for one's ancestors.

In addition to the social aspects of quilt history, the volunteers learned about the quilts' technical and artistic qualities. Some developed special interests: pattern identification, dating of fabric, dyeing and printing of material, designs for quilting. The educational process spread to quilt owners and their families who learned greater appreciation for their quilts, conservation and care, and the importance of considering future disposition of their quilts. In many instances search for ancestral birth and death dates initiated genealogical studies and led owners to uncover diaries, letters, and artifacts that could be handed down as family history along with the quilts.

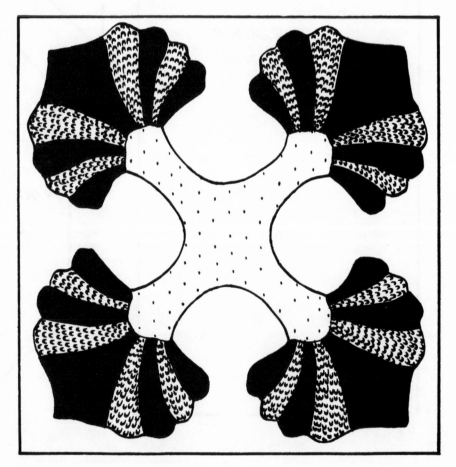

ROCKY MOUNTAIN HONEYSUCKLE
From the family of Elizabeth Llwellyn
Rhea or Meigs County, Tennessee, c. 1900
Red and rose-colored fabric on white cotton.

Some quilt patterns were almost overly popular during certain periods, then diminished in use, perhaps to reappear later. The hexagon is one such pattern with several forms and adaptations. As a single unit, it is called Mosaic and is one of the earliest pieced designs. In the mid-1800s, a circular arrangement of hexagons was called Martha Washington's Flower Garden, and in the twentieth century, Grandmother's Flower Garden. The pattern was seen repeatedly during the survey; almost every quiltmaker of the 1930s and 40s must have made one.

It was always pleasant when a pattern we had not seen before turned up during the survey. Elizabeth Llwellyn owned such a quilt—a delightful example combining pieced and appliquéd work, made about 1900 by a family member. The quilt had been called Rocky Mountain Honeysuckle for as long as Elizabeth could remember. I am not familiar with the botany of the Rockies, but I can vouch for the beauty of the wild honeysuckle in the South.

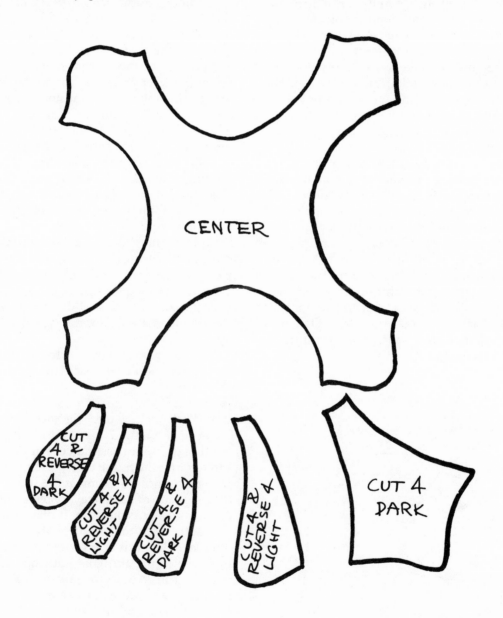

Rocky Mountain Honeysuckle
9-inch block
Piece petals and join to center cross. Then appliqué to a 9-inch square. Add seam allowance to square.

THE QUILTING OF A QUILT

Many people like to piece quilt tops but think quilting the top is a chore. I was a reluctant quilter but eventually discovered what I had been missing. Its rhythmic work, combined with close concentration, has a soothing effect on the body and the mind—a peaceful passage, a refreshing time which can be compared to meditation. There is certainly excitement in cutting pieces and combining colors for quilt blocks but even more excitement when a quilt is finished and taken out of its frame.

When beginning quilters ask "How do I get started?" I often suggest doing a pillow top in the lap without a frame. Quilting in a frame can be mastered later. Good quilting comes with practice and experience so don't expect to be perfect the first week.

Most experts agree that a short needle called a *between* or quilting needle is essential. Size preference varies from a #7 to a #12 depending on the material, the thickness of the quilt, and your dexterity. When a quilt is stretched taut on a frame, it is necessary to go nearly vertical with each stroke of the needle in order to make small, even stitches. In lap quilting with no frame, the motion is horizontal. In frame quilting, the wrist is turned forty-five degrees with each downward stitch and back with each upward stitch in a rocking motion. "Rock your wrist," the instructor says to the beginner.

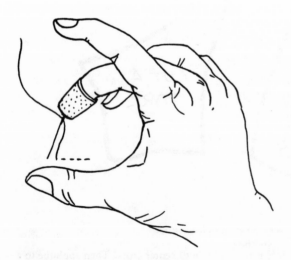

Hand position for quilting in a frame

One finger underneath the quilt must feel each stitch as it is taken to know that the needle has penetrated all three layers of the quilt. Then that finger pushes the quilt up as the upward stitch is taken. Push, release, push, release, over and over again. The left-hand index, middle, and ring fingers may each be used to avoid penetrating a single finger. Some people wear a piece of tape or the tip of an old glove on the finger. A little alum dissolved in water makes a healing dip and toughens the skin.

Another method, two-handed quilting, is accomplished by pushing the needle down all the way through with one hand and returning it with the under hand. Taking one stitch at a time results in a more exact, precise line, which is sometimes desirable. It is also more comfortable for some people with arthritic problems. The running quilting stitch is a smoother, more flowing line. Beware of an occasional back-stitch, "just to fill up space," for it will stand up from the others and make a bump.

Quilters may quilt "in the ditch," that is, directly in the seam. They may quilt "by the piece," around the inside of each piece. They may add richness by quilting double lines. They may vary the concentration of the stitching to change spaces and shapes. Skimpy quilting barely gets by.

Not everyone has room to set up a quilting frame, but don't let that deter you. There are alternatives.

The Whole Quilt Basted Together
For this method I recommend going to a quilting group for assistance. Put the back, filler, and top into the frame tautly, as though you were going to quilt it. Starting at the frame edge, do a thorough job of basting every ten inches or so up, down, and across the quilt. It may be necessary to roll both sides to complete the basting in the middle. When it is completely basted, remove it from the frame and take your quilt home with you. You may wish to quilt it in a rectangular, round, or oval frame, or you may choose to lay it on a table and quilt it loose.

If no frame for basting is available, the quilt can be laid out on the floor, taping the backing down or pinning it to carpet. Proceed as before to baste all three layers together.

Quarter-Sized Quilting

Instead of completely joining the top, leave it in four quarters and quilt these units as lap quilting, in a frame or not.

A rectangular rug-hooking frame, if you happen to have one, makes a satisfactory quilting frame for sectional or baby quilts. Then sew completed sections together by seaming the unjoined edges of the quilt top. Spread the quilt out (upside down), trim away any excess batting, overlap the backing, turn under one edge, and blind-stitch into position. Some top stitching may be added at the joining edge to complete the quilting pattern.

Lap-Quilting

Quilting individual blocks is a convenient method for some people. Each block is put together with batting and backing and quilted singly. Then the blocks are joined using the preceding method.

Basting the three layers together

Frame Quilting

My favorite method of quilting requires a full-sized floor frame. It is always there, ready for a few moments of work or an all-day session.

Putting a quilt in a frame is quite easy and can be accomplished in an hour or less when you have had a little experience. The frame I use is made of four pieces of wood approximately 96 x 1 x 2 inches. The ends are clamped together with C-clamps to form a rectangle. The frame rests on legs, but saw horses or chair backs can be used. Each side of the frame has a 2-inch strip of cloth attached along its length.

I suggest the following procedures for frame quilting. Have the pre-washed quilt back extend about two inches beyond the edges of the top, making sure all edges are cut straight. With the wrong side up, pin and baste one long side of the back to the frame's basting strip. Do the same to the opposite side. Basting stitches need not be small.

Pin the two ends of the backing to the frame's basting strips or to strips of cloth tied at 8-inch intervals along the end frames. (The ends are not basted in because the quilt will need to be unfastened and rolled in the quilting process.) The back should be truly square and taut, but not stretched overly tight.

Spread the batting carefully over the back. It can be slightly smaller than the size of the back so as to extend an inch beyond the edges of the quilt top. Next, place the top on the frame, making sure it is squared with the frame and the corners are true. Baste all around the edge of the top.

If the frame is to be left extended for quilting, additional basting is not required. If the quilt is to be rolled to a narrower width before quilting or taken down at intervals, baste in vertical and horizontal rows about ten inches apart to make an allover grid with long, galloping stitches. The quilt can be rolled as basting progresses toward the center.

Use this same method of basting with tops to be quilted in a hoop or small frame. There will be no wrinkles on the back as so often happens in floor basting.

The Quilting Design

I am frequently asked, "How am I going to quilt my top?" My answer is to wait until it is basted into the frame. Not all quiltmakers will agree, but to me it is very important to place the backing, filler, and top together before making that decision. The top will settle into the bulk of the batting to make shapes of its own accord. Instead of imposing yourself on the quilt, see if you can let the quilt tell you what to do. You can become sensitive to the forms and make your design fit them. Study the assembled quilt to discover the predominant lines. Think of the quilting pattern as an opposing design to the main pattern. Think of a line drawing over a wash drawing. The mounds and forms will give you clues to quilting lines.

When a quilt is made of squares and rectangles, curving lines may provide pleasing variety. (See page 4.) When blocks are vertical and horizontal, a diagonal quilting line may improve the rhythm. Some blocks may need to be quilted around each piece to accent the block and bring out the design.

Vary the scale of the quilting so some areas are more closely quilted than others. (See page 29).

The surface will be richer for it. Try to plan a different way of quilting for each quilt. A simple design may be more beautiful than one with complicated shapes that fail to allow for pleasing mounds of light and shadow. Remember that the quilting line will become a valley and make forms in relief. Study quilts to find patterns you consider most successful. You will learn to appreciate the variety and suitability of different designs.

For your own quilting designs, cut several shapes from folded paper. Choose the best one to outline on stiff paper, cardboard, or plastic.

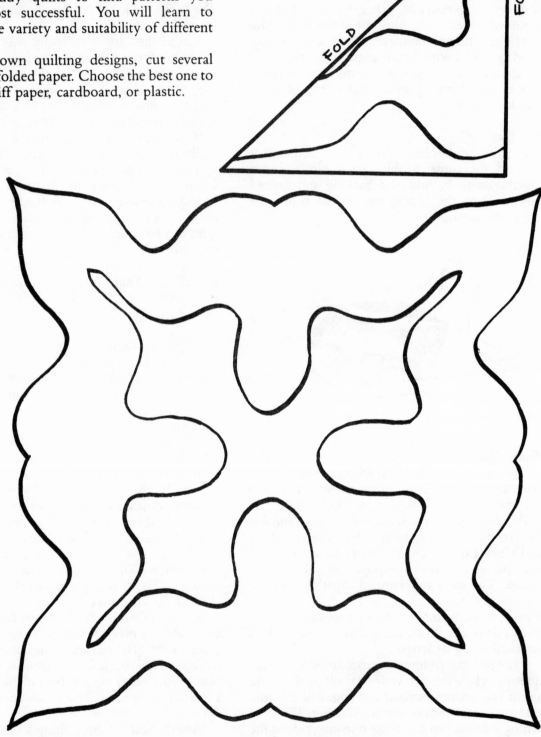

Cutting a quilting pattern

Marking may be done with a non-greasy pencil. A thin-line #3 mechanical pencil mark will virtually disappear during the quilting process. A kneaded or artgum eraser will clean up any remains. Many a good quilter will outline with her needle and follow the mark or put a few pins around the pattern shape as a guide.

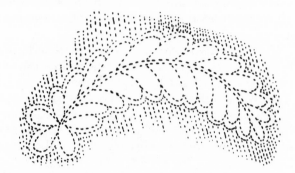

Close quilting on a nineteenth-century quilt

Mark dark fabric with white colored pencil or a sliver of soap. "Disappearing" pencils are suspect, as they may leave a harmful chemical residue. Some quilters like to use ¼-inch masking tape as a guide for straight lines, but I prefer to let my eye be the guide. (Masking tape should not be left on the cloth for any lengthy period of time.) Cutting designs from Contact paper and laying the pattern on the quilt to stitch around provides yet another method. (Again, remove it promptly.) As a quilter, you will develop your own way of doing things and will gather ideas from other quiltmakers. No one has all the answers; we all learn from each other.

The Art of Quilting

The piecing and appliquéing of quilts is an art, and many quiltmakers are gifted artists who choose wonderful colors and create outstanding designs. Their work is not completed, however, until the top has been quilted. With quilting, new forms emerge; the contours resulting from the quilting complement or accentuate the pattern of the patchwork top.

Until recent years, when polyester filler was developed, cotton or wool batting was generally used. Many people still remember picking cotton, taking it to gin, and carding it into batts for quiltmaking. Those who raised sheep made fleece into batts. Ready-made batts could also be purchased or ordered by catalog and "Mountain Mist" was a familiar household word. Since the cotton batt was not bonded or locked in any way,

close quilting was required to keep the fibers from balling up during laundering.

Contemporary quilters appreciate synthetic batting, for it is easy to sew through, lightweight yet warm, holds its shape, does not migrate, and washes well. Polyester-filled quilts look puffier; and their contours are rounder. Old quilting designs like the feathered wreath, created when only cotton batting was in use, tend to look stiff and somewhat mashed when stitched into polyester batting.

Consider, then, the kind of batting you are using when you plan the quilting design. For synthetic batting, choose a pattern that will allow the puffiness to accent the total design. With good quality synthetic batting, it will not be necessary to do the close quilting cotton requires. If you are quilting an antique or pre-1950s top, it will not look authentic unless you use a cotton or eighty-percent cotton batt available at some fabric shops and many quilt stores.

Study every quilt you see and concentrate on the way it is quilted. Decide what is good about it, what might have made it better. Doing so will enrich your plans for future projects.

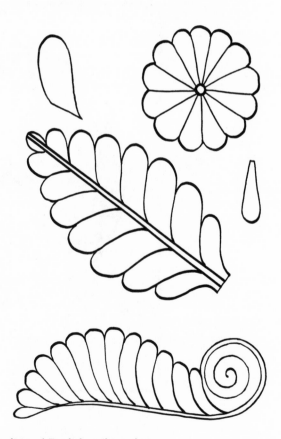

Traditional English quilting designs

Confederate Basket: *A Fund-Raising Quilt*

Everyone who has seen Pat Ferrero's film, *Quilts in Women's Lives,* has thoroughly enjoyed it. Pat asked me to serve as consultant when she made a second film on the subject: *Hearts and Hands: A Social History of Nineteenth-Century Women and Quilts.* She especially wanted to know how quiltmaking was used for fund-raising and patriotic purposes in the Civil War period. I had read a few women's Civil War diaries, and I supplemented that information with several pleasant hours of reading in university and state libraries studying nineteenth-century women's diaries, letters, and account books.

I learned that women of the Raus community near Shelbyville, Tennessee, made several basket-pattern quilts as fund-raisers for Confederate forces. The women inscribed their own names with ink on the quilts as well as those of some volunteers serving in the army. Mary High Prince, one of the quilts' makers, was also a Confederate spy who narrowly escaped the death

penalty on one occasion when captured. Many years later she made a patchwork pillow from squares of the homespun she and her friends had worn during the blockade. Fittingly, she owned one of the fund-raising quilts, and it has remained in her family to this day.

Through my research I learned firsthand how many lives changed in a very short time during the war. The diary of Myra Inman Carter of Cleveland, Tennessee, began when she was a beautiful young belle, one of four well-provided-for sisters who had a delightful social and family life. An early entry of February 1859, at about age fourteen states, "A rainy day. I have been sewing all day on Sister's basket quilt." A week later she wrote, "Been piecing quilts, finished one, commenced another."

By early 1861, volunteers were leaving for duty. Knitting and sewing for military personnel became a part of women's lives. August 5, 1861, "Florence Johnson and Mrs. Montgomery were

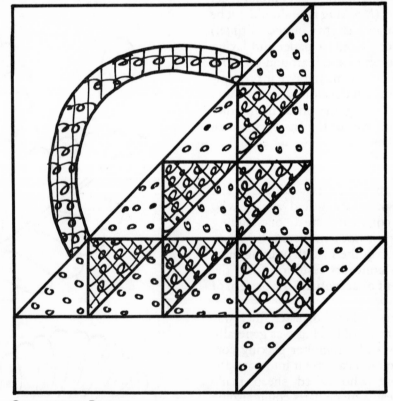

CONFEDERATE BASKET
Makers: Women of the Raus community, Bedford County, Tennessee, including Mary High Prince, 1863–1864
Assorted fabrics set together with white cotton fabric.

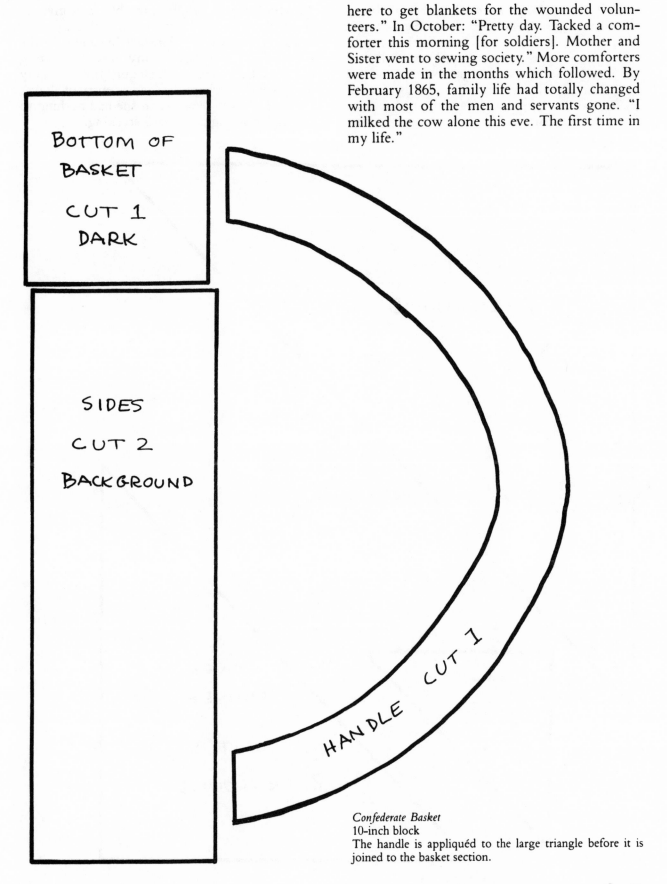

here to get blankets for the wounded volunteers." In October: "Pretty day. Tacked a comforter this morning [for soldiers]. Mother and Sister went to sewing society." More comforters were made in the months which followed. By February 1865, family life had totally changed with most of the men and servants gone. "I milked the cow alone this eve. The first time in my life."

BOTTOM OF BASKET

CUT 1 DARK

SIDES CUT 2 BACKGROUND

HANDLE CUT 1

Confederate Basket
10-inch block
The handle is appliquéd to the large triangle before it is joined to the basket section.

Dolly Lunt Burge was widowed in 1850 and left to manage a plantation in middle Georgia. With numerous field hands, house servants and a competent overseer, she managed very well until the war. Eventually, she lost the overseer and had to assume agricultural duties as well as those of the house. In the pre-war days she had written that a quilting party at Mrs. Perry's was a pleasure but by November 1864, she wrote, "Warped and dressed the loom. Oh, how this blockade gives us work for all hands." Eventually, with only a few aging Negroes left, "Finished breaking up the Pine field . . . ploughing my garden, planting potatoes, beets, etc. . . . Felt quite tired with my day's work." Perhaps the saddest entry of all was Christmas Eve, 1864, when she had nothing to put in her young daughter's stocking.

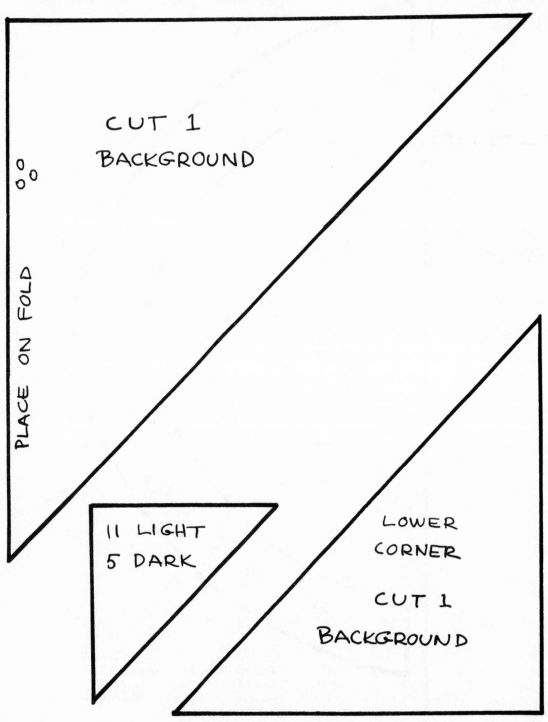

CUT 1
BACKGROUND

PLACE ON FOLD

11 LIGHT
5 DARK

LOWER
CORNER

CUT 1
BACKGROUND

Tennessee Wild Rose: *A Pieced Pattern*

Southern quiltmakers have long had a preference for floral motifs, both pieced and appliquéd. Many of the "best quilts," those handed down for generations, are of floral design. Young women preparing for marriage bought new material and chose a special pattern to show off their sewing skills.

One such quilt, judging by its 112 x 122-inch measurements, was apparently designed for a high tester bed. It wasn't as outstanding as many of the Rose-of-Sharon quilts of the period, but I was impressed by its size and the fact that it looked different from other appliqué quilts. Each 10-inch block made of a single red rose with four buds alternated with a plain white block of equal size. The tan center of the rose had probably faded from a light red. The quilt's borderless edge was bound in red.

"A simple, somewhat primitive appliquéd rose," I thought. "Too bad the maker didn't have a little more imagination when she designed her block."

Then I inspected the quilt more closely and found this was not an appliqué quilt at all. Roses and buds were pieced with background material to make the block, not *laid on* the background as in appliqué work.

Joining curved pieces and making them fit together calls for great skill. Whoever made this quilt set herself quite a task. I was intrigued.

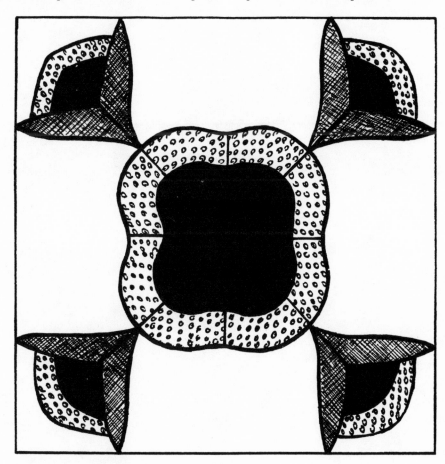

TENNESSEE WILD ROSE
  Maker: Mahala P. Batey
  Rutherford County, Tennessee, c. 1850
  Rose solid faded to tan, Turkey red, and green, with white cotton fabric.

None of my reference books showed similar quilts, so I sent a description and drawing of the pattern to several friends for comparison.

Cuesta Benberry of St. Louis replied almost at once. My rose quilt was similar to one made in Iowa about 1850 that she had purchased some twenty years earlier. Examining hers closely, she discovered hers, too, was pieced. She had been told her quilt was a Roses and Buds or Combination Rose. A similar example in the Oklahoma Historical Society's book, *A Century of Quilts,* is called California Rose (Oklahoma Historical Society, 2100 Lincoln Blvd., Oklahoma City, OK 73105). Quilter's Rose is the name given in the St. Louis area. According to information we have gathered, pieced-rose construction seems to have been used only during the mid-1800s.

If you decide to make this version of a pieced-rose quilt, I hope you will add an attractive border. It could be an appliquéd trailing vine, several bands of harmonizing colors, a wide band of a handsome drapery or slipcover print in the style of the South Carolina *broderie perse* quilts, or a wide strip of the background material embellished with a fancy quilting design. Whatever your border, it will make your rose garden ever so much prettier.

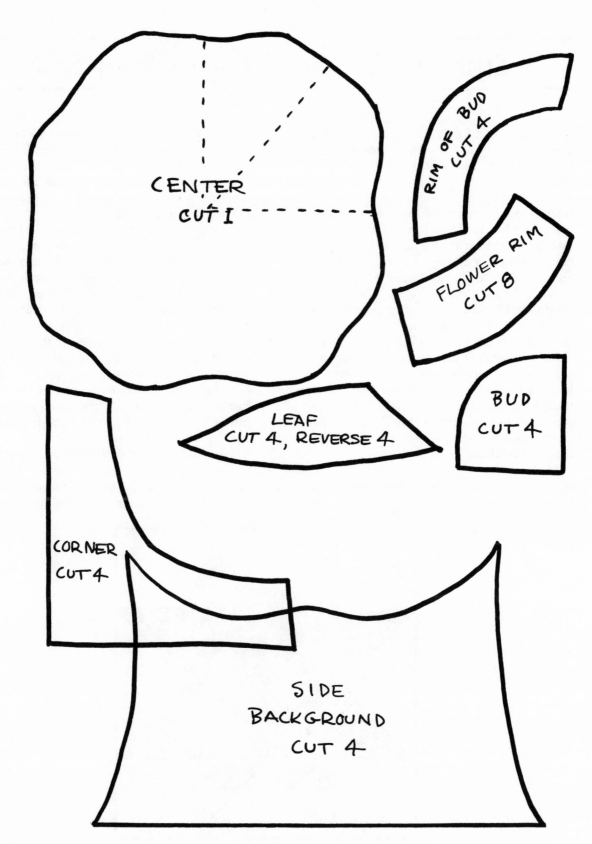

CENTER
CUT 1

RIM OF BUD
CUT 4

FLOWER RIM
CUT 8

BUD
CUT 4

LEAF
CUT 4, REVERSE 4

CORNER
CUT 4

SIDE
BACKGROUND
CUT 4

Tennessee Wild Rose
10-inch block, all pieced
The center, in wedge shapes, can be pieced to the rim pieces
and then joined to make the flower.

String-Quilt Star: *A Use for Every Scrap*

✦

One day I met Laura Blevins, a Chattanoogan, who told me how she took Tennessee quiltmaking to Africa. Laura and her husband, C. E. Blevins, spent five years in Kitwe, Zambia, Africa, as Baptist missionaries. She invited an international mixture of African, French, German, East Indian, Danish, and Canadian women into her home for classes and fellowship. Six or eight women, ranging in age from sixteen to eighty-four, usually came once a week.

When Laura learned that in Zambia even the shoddiest blanket cost eighty dollars and that some cover was needed most of the year, she decided to teach quiltmaking. A Canadian missionary loaned her some patterns and books, and she set out to buy large bundles of scraps from a local garment factory. These narrow scraps were usually in long pieces, just right for string-quilt piecing. Later, American churches sent boxes of cloth, allowing the women more diversity in their quiltmaking.

Most of the women knew how to sew, and some were unusually accomplished in embroidery. They learned quiltmaking quickly, but one

woman from a northern province had never held a needle or pair of scissors in her hand. It took her most of one day to cut out four squares; eventually, she completed a quilt of which she was most proud, although it might not have borne close inspection.

Laura started everyone on a string quilt, cutting squares of newspaper for pattern foundations and seaming strips of cloth onto the paper. After the edges were trimmed and the paper removed, the women seamed their blocks together. Fortunately, Laura had brought a large roll of batting with her to Africa; so each person had enough filler for one quilt. Some were tacked, others quilted. After that, quilts were merely lined or used to cover flimsy blankets and give them longer life. String piecing was used for Fan and Star quilts after the initial string-pieced square was made. One woman added lace to her fans for embellishment.

The women who lived in the town of Kitwe had relatively comfortable homes, but those in outlying areas lived in block houses or huts, slept on mats placed on the floor, and had little or no

STRING-QUILT STAR
Maker: Pamona Louvicy Forester Stuart
Hickman County, Tennessee, c. 1893
Assorted scraps with blue background, red strips for set.

furniture. Their quilts gave them a sense of luxury.

Laura Blevins may not have been a dedicated quiltmaker when she left the United States, but she found a new calling. She provided fellowship and warmth, and her students enjoyed accomplishing a worthy task.

String quilts have been a tradition in the South for a long time. Economy-minded women have used the smallest, narrowest of scraps to make colorful, charming quilts using the string-quilt method. In addition to plain squares and stars, the technique has been used for Kite, Fan, Rocky Road to Kansas, and Spider Web patterns as well as shapes within the North Carolina Lily, Tulip pattern or One Thousand Triangles pattern. You can adapt string-quilt piecing to any quilt pattern with colorful results admirably suited to everyday use.

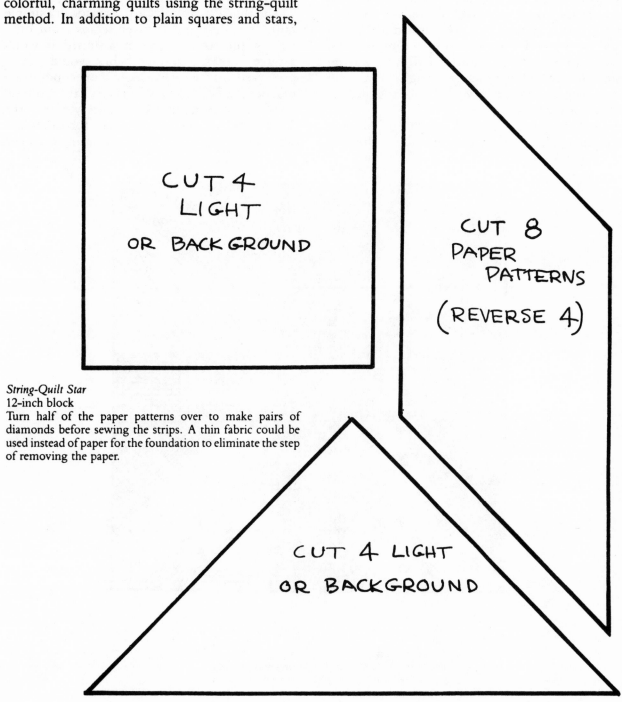

String-Quilt Star
12-inch block
Turn half of the paper patterns over to make pairs of diamonds before sewing the strips. A thin fabric could be used instead of paper for the foundation to eliminate the step of removing the paper.

Blue Patchwork Cross: *A Two-Generation Effort*

When Pamona Louvicy Forester married Milton Stuart in 1890, she assumed the many duties required of a farmer's wife in Sugar Creek, Hickman County, Tennessee. "Monie" and her husband spent several years building a handsome two-story house with porches on the front of both stories enclosed by well-turned bannisters and fretwork. The couple worked together long hours to achieve their goals, and there was no time for restful quilting, although Monie did complete a Blue Patchwork Cross top shortly after her marriage.

In 1930, at the age of seventeen, Monie's daughter, Bertha May, married Roe J. Boulton

against the wishes of her parents and took her mother's patchwork quilt top as part of her dowry. She devoted her life to sharing the responsibilities of a farmer's wife, raising a family of five, and finishing her mother's project.

The Blue Patchwork Cross is made in a simple, humble style using leftover scraps from other sewing projects. Its maker assumed it would receive hard use and probably would not be preserved as a family heirloom. For economy and practicality, Southern quiltmakers have produced hundreds of string quilts in a variety of patterns. The "strings," scraps too small for other use, were the narrow strips left from cutting garments

BLUE PATCHWORK CROSS
   Makers: Pamona Louvicy Forester Stuart and Bertha May
Stuart Boulton
   Hickman County, Tennessee, c. 1895, 1930
   Assorted cotton scraps set with black-and-white check strips and red squares and dark blue strips with green squares. (See cover illustration.)

and other large shapes. Monie's quilt was constructed in the following way.

Using a 5 x 5-inch square of newspaper or other scrap paper as a piecing foundation, she placed a small scrap right side up at one corner of the square. Then she added a strip, right side down, on top of the first scrap along its inner edge, seaming the two edges together through the two layers and the paper. She opened up and flattened out the second scrap and applied a third strip in the same way. When she had covered the paper square completely, she trimmed away any excess material from the edges and pressed the block. Lastly, she removed the paper, and her block was ready to be assembled with others like it.

Monie used a fine black and white checked strip, 2½-inches wide, to set four squares together with a red square at the crossing. She put these blocks together with a strip of dark blue, 2¾ inches wide, with green at the crossing. Her double grid created the illusion of in-and-out movement in the design and produced an outstanding example of a simple quilt.

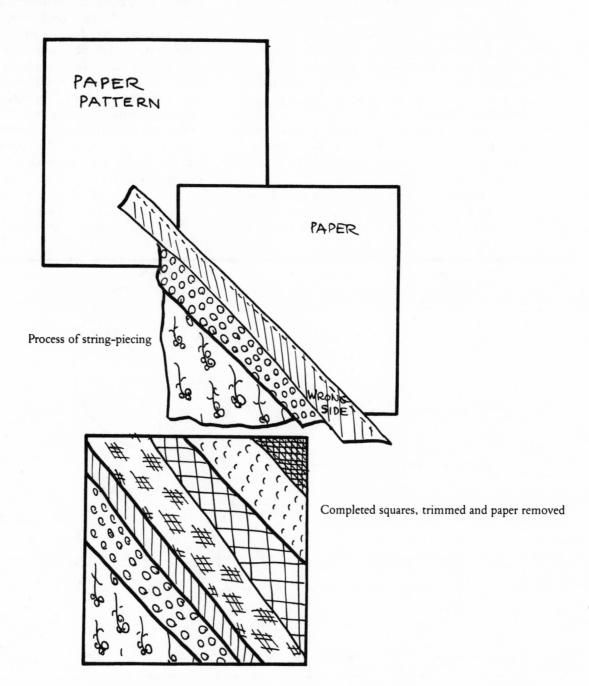

Process of string-piecing

Completed squares, trimmed and paper removed

COLOR FOR QUILTERS

A quilter can never know too much about color. Many artists have spent their entire lives studying the meaning and uses of color. Josef Albers, a member of the Bauhaus artists group who taught at Yale for many years, did numerous paintings of squares within squares to demonstrate the subtlety of color relationships. It is little wonder, then, that quilters seldom find a short course in color.

One of the easiest ways to learn about the workings of color doesn't require a book or a teacher. You can see for yourself by making several versions of one block in different combinations of fabric and color. How does light work against dark? What does an all-pastel block look like? What effect do all-prints or all-solids have on a design? What happens when you put red next to blue? Why do some colors move in, others out? How does color affect mood? You will learn something about contrast, accent, busyness, intensity, texture, suitability and personal taste if you can "read" your experiments.

Examples may be stitched in patchwork or in fabric pieces pasted together to demonstrate various possibilities.

Choosing Color

A quilter may have mastered the techniques of quiltmaking but still feel uncertain when making color choices. No matter how fine the work and how dynamic the design, an unsuccessful color combination will negate a quilt's good points. The individual with a naive understanding of color can be distinguished from one who knows the need for contrast, repetition, accent, and other elements of design.

Because of uncertainty, beginning quilters tend to choose one range of colors for their first quilts. There is nothing wrong with such a choice; it is a safe way to develop a design. The quilter may use browns, tans, and gold for a cozy-looking quilt or may prefer the cool look of blue shades.

A one-color (monochromatic) quilt is a good place to start, and fabric shops have wonderful

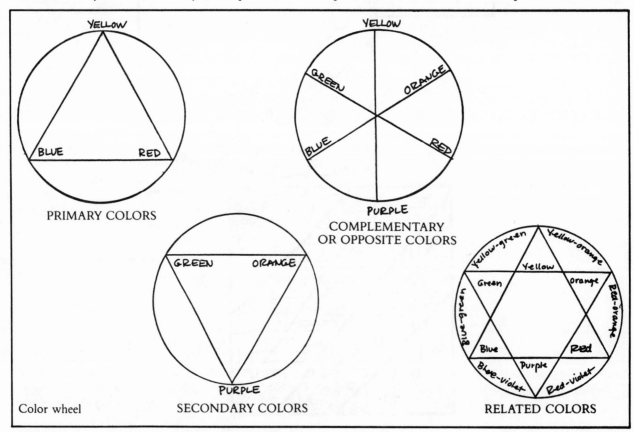

Color wheel

PRIMARY COLORS

COMPLEMENTARY OR OPPOSITE COLORS

SECONDARY COLORS

RELATED COLORS

arrays of color-coordinated material waiting for the eager quilter. All the cloth matches because designers have made it so; in the end, however, the quilter's personal touch may be lacking.

From the one-color quilt, try introducing the use of color opposites (complementary colors). If the first quilt was done in rust, peach, tan, and brown, try adding some blue for a bit of spice. The blue can be muted or grayed, not full-color intensity, to offer a pleasing contrast. Experiment with leftover scraps from earlier work. See how the addition of the opposite color changes the appearance of the predominant color.

Sew or paste a block made from one-color scraps. Add a bit of the opposite color, or complement, to see how the color relationship changes. Pin your block up and look at it occasionally.

Orange and blue, red and green, yellow and purple opposites do not need to be used in full strength. They can be light, dark, or grayed down to soft tones, yet still brighten or intensify your main color. Adding opposites will do for your quilt what pepper does for oyster stew.

Try your color experiments as single blocks to be finished as future gifts or, if you want to speed along, make paste-up blocks with fabric glued on paper. In the latter case, cut the quilt pieces without a seam allowance. Use a glue-stick to put your pieces on the paper. Choose a pattern with several shapes to allow for the use of four or five fabrics.

Color Harmony and Balance

Having considered what happens when the complement is added to one-color or monochromatic quilts, we must next look for harmony in color design. You achieve harmony when your colors balance each other.

When you look at a color, your eye expects to see the opposite of that color. Remember the after-image exercise you did in science class of looking at a red square, then covering the eye and seeing green? Your eye completes the balance by creating the complementary color. Balance, or harmony, is one of the essentials of successful quilt design.

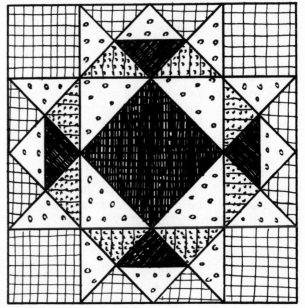

Georgetown Circle

Red, yellow, and blue comprise the three primary colors of the color wheel. Their opposites, which "finish" or balance them, are called secondary, or complementary, colors. Green balances red; orange balances blue and purple balances yellow. Any color can be lightened or darkened by adding white or black—or grayed by adding a bit of its complement.

More experiments will help you understand further the messages of color. Pin or tape your trial blocks to the wall or bulletin board; studying them over a period of time will help you decide which are most successful, which please you the most.

Choose a block like Jacob's Ladder or Georgetown Circle. Use one of the primary colors—red, yellow, or blue—in four different fabrics of plain, print, light, and dark. This is a primary, one-color-design block.

Jacob's Ladder

For the second experiment, use some of the same fabric but add one fabric in the complement to that color, as you did in your earlier problem. Choose judiciously, considering subdued or pale tones as well as those of full intensity. This is a design with complementary colors.

For the third problem, take two of the fabrics used in your first trial, the primary color block, and add a color next to that color on the wheel. If blue is the primary color used, choose purple or green. Add one or both of the adjacent colors to the primary color. This is called an analogous combination, one in which colors have similarity.

Another trial block can be made as a lesson in discipline. Take the color you are least fond of and do one of the above exercises. It will help you become better acquainted with that color and you may grow to like it.

Black and White Drama

Do you ever include black in your quiltmaking? Perhaps you have been omitting an important ingredient because you have not become acquainted with its properties.

In the Victorian era, people wore black and gray clothing for a rather extended period after the death of a loved one. When the mourning period ceased, the dark clothing fabrics sometimes went into the making of a quilt. Hours spent in the process allowed for memories to surge and healing to occur.

Amish and Mennonite quilters have long favored the use of black in their quilts to intensify and give greater depth and contrast to their strong, clear colors. Even small amounts of black will change the whole character of a color combination.

Adding black, white, gray, and all their variations to your color vocabulary will help you achieve a more refined perception of color in your quiltmaking.

Lois Hall, who once lived on an East Tennessee farm (now covered by Tellico Lake), utilized black and white to accent the brighter colors of her Swing in the Center quilt. She used lively prints, each block a different material, and combined them with black and white fabric. As a result, a grid of black directs the eye movement from one diagonal line of color to another. The relationship of dark, light, and color seems in perfect balance. (See color illustration.)

Here are more color problems to solve.
1. Make a block without color, using black,

white, and gray. Fabrics may be prints and/or solids in any combination.
2. Take two or three fabrics in different colors. Add white or an off-white and make a sample block. Weathervane, Goose in the Pond, Northumberland Star, or Golgotha are possible choices of design.
3. Make the same block and substitute black in place of the white.

Put your blocks where you can see them at odd moments. Just as you enter the room, you may see that a certain fabric isn't quite right. Subtract and add until you get the right combination. Soon you will begin to see that some colors are successful while other combinations are less so. Work to achieve the design which pleases you; the result will be worth the extra effort and time.

Swing in the Center as made by Lois Hall

The Need for Contrast

To the study of balance we must relate contrast. We have learned that complementary colors and black and white give contrast. We can see other ways of providing contrast through the following experiment.
1. Choose a give-and-take pattern like Robbing Peter to Pay Paul or the Drunkard's Path in which colors are reversed in adjacent squares. Make two units and reverse the colors in two more using two complementary colors (red and green or orange and blue). The colors will vibrate against each other if used in equal intensity. There may

be times when you wish to create such tension, and other times when you want to avoid it. Knowing this interaction should help you achieve your color goals.

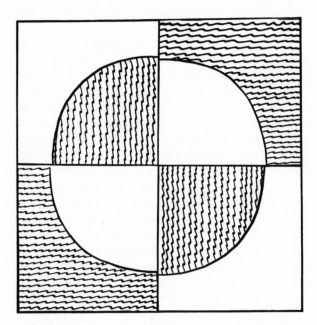

Drunkard's Path

2. Make the same grouping using one of the first colors and a lighter shade of the second to produce a more compatible combination; more contrast and less tension result.
3. Select three or four fabrics in different colors ranging from light to dark. Make three blocks using a simple pattern like Monkey Wrench. Change the position of colors in each of the blocks and compare the effects. Which has the most contrast? The least? If your choices don't please you, substitute other material.

The contrast of light and dark, subdued and strong colors gives life to the design. Movement of the eye from light to dark and from pale to strong creates a certain rhythm. Lack of contrast bores the eye and fails the imagination. Prints scaled too similarly lead to monotony, also. Look for a change in size of patterning on your printed fabrics to insure maximum design quality.

When you look at the finished blocks, is there one that bounces too much? See what you can do to remedy it, or try another combination. There is no such thing as bad color; it is what you do with it that matters.

The Power of Color

As you study your blocks, you will begin to see how some colors move toward you while some seem to go away. Warm colors like red, orange, and yellow catch your attention; cool blues, greens, and violets seem to recede. Colors can affect feelings and moods. Red and orange seem to cause excitement, while blue and green are restful. Use the same pattern as before or select another one for the next experiments.

1. Make a block using warm colors. Make the same block using cool colors. How would the block look if it had a light center or if a black border were added? Add and subtract from the blocks until you get the arrangement which pleases you most.
2. Gather a group of your friends—perhaps your sewing or quilt group. Ask each person to bring a bag containing a few quilt scraps. Exchange the unopened bags and make a quilt block with someone else's choice of colors. You may discover some new ways of combining fabric that hadn't occurred to you.

By now you should be confident enough to make color work for you. Refer to your experiments from time to time to remind yourself of color's many possibilities.

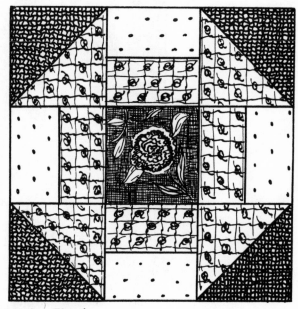

Monkey Wrench

Southern Charm: *Working toward Color Harmony*

Exchanging friendship blocks is one of the pleasant customs among quiltmakers. In nineteenth-century Maryland, competition for artistic appliquéd squares became so fierce that some less-talented women hired professional quiltmakers to do their work. The exchange of blocks among these women resulted in the wonderful Baltimore album quilts so highly prized today.

We know that young ladies of the Victorian era also swapped fabric and squares for crazy quilts. They put together these pieces and blocks with a remarkable assortment of embroidery stitches, giving evidence of their level of accomplishment.

A third kind of exchange required the quiltmaker to obtain material from her friends for the making of a one-patch quilt; no two pieces of fabric could be alike. Called a *Charm quilt,* the custom itself has charm. A number of shapes suit the Charm quilt. One shape, called *Charm,* is also known as Double-Headed Axe. Odd Fellow, Diamond, Mosaic, Pyramids, Tumbler, Clam Shell, Brickwork, Coffin, Honeycomb, and Postage Stamp patterns also fit the Charm quilt idea. Even Yo-Yo, Cathedral Window, and Biscuit quilts can be Charm quilts.

Once you have chosen a shape, consider the total concept of your quilt. If the pieces are put together as they accumulate, what sort of color harmony will emerge? Is it possible to arrange lights and darks to make a more orderly design, as in Pyramids, where light triangles point down and dark triangles up? Alternate rows of clam shells can be light and dark. Horizontal Double-Headed Axe pieces can be light, vertical ones dark, and so on. A Charm quilt with no regard for color placement lacks the dynamics of good design. (A picture of Southern Charm appears among the colored photographs of this book.)

One teacher who made quilts was given scraps by her schoolchildren and their parents. A bus commuter pieced blocks donated by regular riders. Since each scrap was of a different

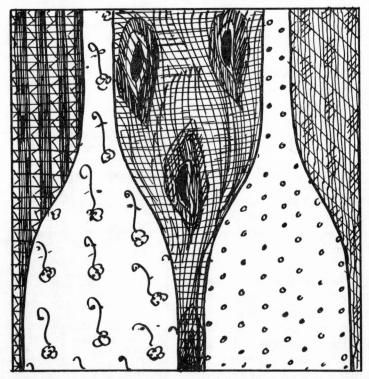

SOUTHERN CHARM
Designer and maker: the author
Chattanooga, Tennessee, 1985–1987
American and English cotton prints and solids, cream-colored border.

material, the work of an invalid Civil War veteran in his Brick Wall quilt serves as a prime record of the printed calicos of the period. Today quilt groups have scrap day for swapping materials.

Southern Charm is a new one-block design that I based on the Ogee shape found throughout art history. If it looks like a bottle to you, that is all right, too.

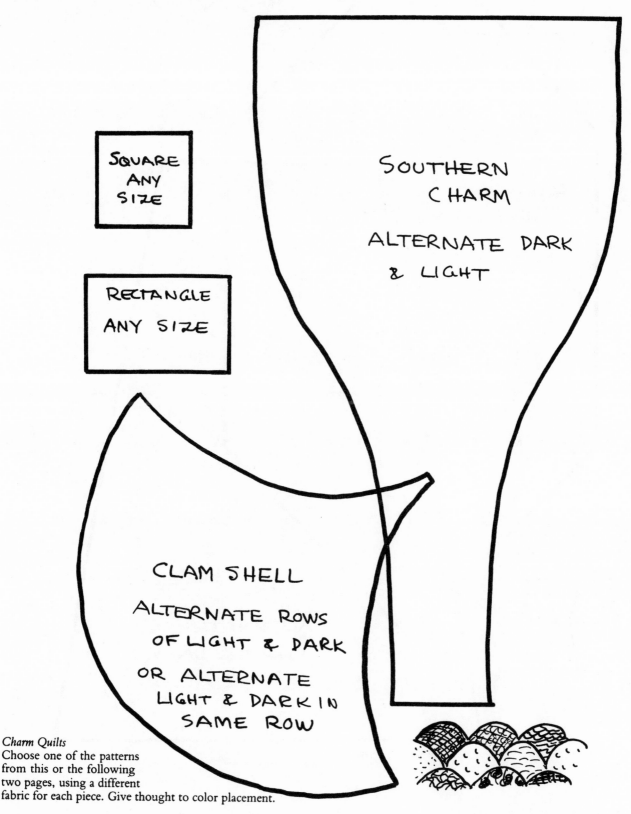

SQUARE ANY SIZE

RECTANGLE ANY SIZE

SOUTHERN CHARM

ALTERNATE DARK & LIGHT

CLAM SHELL

ALTERNATE ROWS OF LIGHT & DARK

OR ALTERNATE LIGHT & DARK IN SAME ROW

Charm Quilts
Choose one of the patterns from this or the following two pages, using a different fabric for each piece. Give thought to color placement.

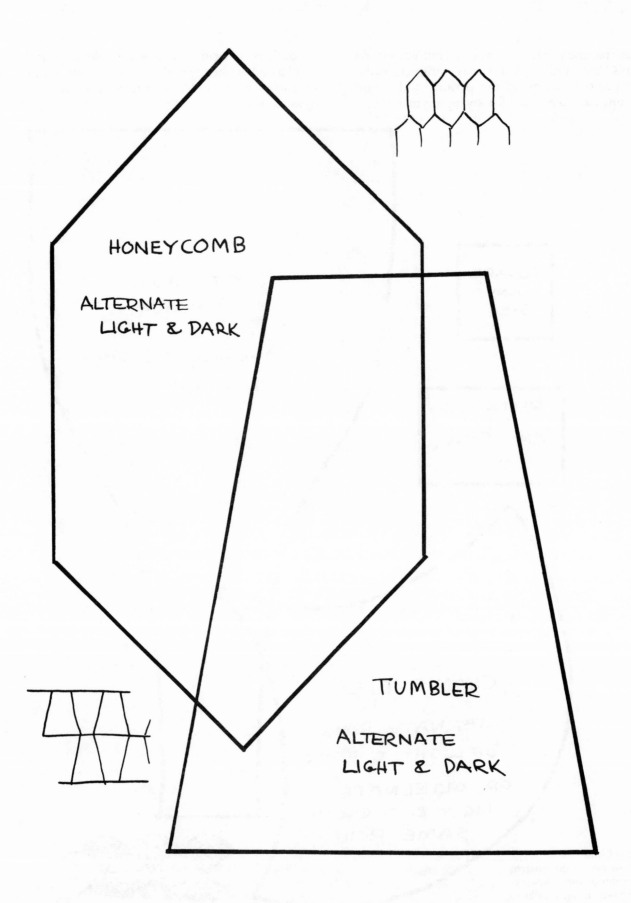

HONEYCOMB

ALTERNATE
LIGHT & DARK

TUMBLER

ALTERNATE
LIGHT & DARK

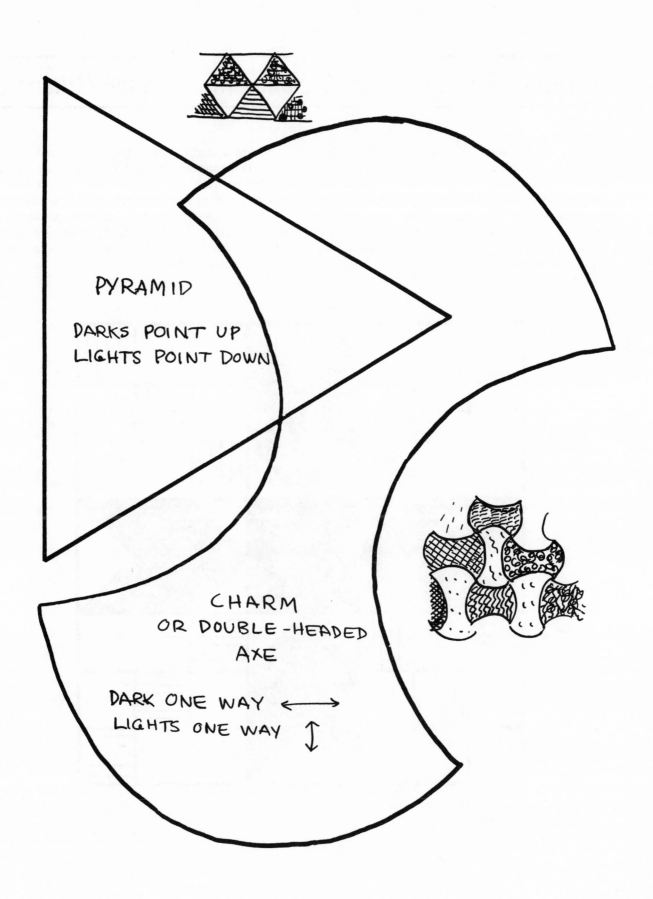

PYRAMID

DARKS POINT UP
LIGHTS POINT DOWN

CHARM
OR DOUBLE-HEADED
AXE

DARK ONE WAY ←→
LIGHTS ONE WAY ↕

Indian Arrowhead: *A Southern Heritage Pattern*

❖

The Indian Arrowhead pattern and a variant, Arrowhead Star, are reminders of the past—tributes to the native Americans who inhabited the South's myriad landscapes long before Hernando deSoto or Daniel Boone traveled here. The pattern's sharply angular motif was found during the two-year study of the quilts of Tennessee, although the pattern is by no means exclusive to that state.

Using a traditional Nine Patch format, early quilters arranged the block's six basic geometric shapes to highlight its four arrowheads which converge at the center square. The Thursday Bee of the Smoky Mountain Quilters included a sampler Arrowhead block in their Tennessee Heritage quilt pictured among the colored photographs in this book.

INDIAN ARROWHEAD
Maker: unknown
Meigs County, Tennessee, c. 1880
Assorted scraps, primarily brown, with white background cotton fabric.

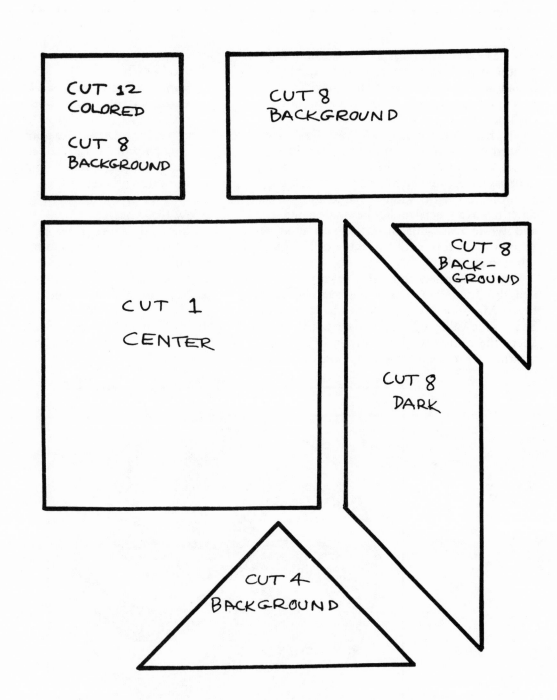

Indian Arrowhead
12-inch block
The outer triangle can be placed with a seam down the center, if preferred, by using the inner triangle pattern.

Naomi's Pinwheel: *Using Balance in Design*

It has been my pleasure to see hundreds of Southern quilts since my study of quiltmaking began sixteen years ago. They have been old, new, perfect, flawed, colorful or subdued and each has had a character all its own.

My next door neighbor showed me a quilt handed down in her family for more than 100 years. Made by Naomi Griffith of Cedar Springs, Tennessee, before she married, the quilt edge is embroidered with Naomi's name and the date. Since it was a special quilt, one single print, a blue and white resist-dot material, was used with white for the top, with a backing of handwoven white material.

Family members through the years have valued the quilt, laundering it enough to keep it fresh. Many of Naomi's descendants remain in Sequatchie Valley where she lived; family custom keeps the cemetery plot in order, but years and weather wear the stones away and in time this lovely quilt may be the only remaining evidence of Naomi's life.

Its major design feature is a round, curving pinwheel thirteen inches in diameter. Plain white surrounds seven blue and seven white segments; thirty wheels make up the quilt. The liveliness of swirling pinwheels is contained by restful areas of white. Its quilting is meticulously executed in the background with a simple cross-hatching pattern and on the pieced blocks by close lines which follow the wheel.

Blue and white resist-prints were popular quiltmaking fabrics in Naomi's day. To my way of thinking, nothing is more handsome than a crisp, clean, blue and white quilt with plenty of good quilting. Be warned, though, that the Spinning Ball is not easy to make. (A color photograph of a pinwheel block appears with other colored photographs in this book.)

NAOMI'S PINWHEEL
Maker: Naomi Griffith Daniel
Sequatchie County, Tennessee, 1841
Blue and white cotton print with white background.

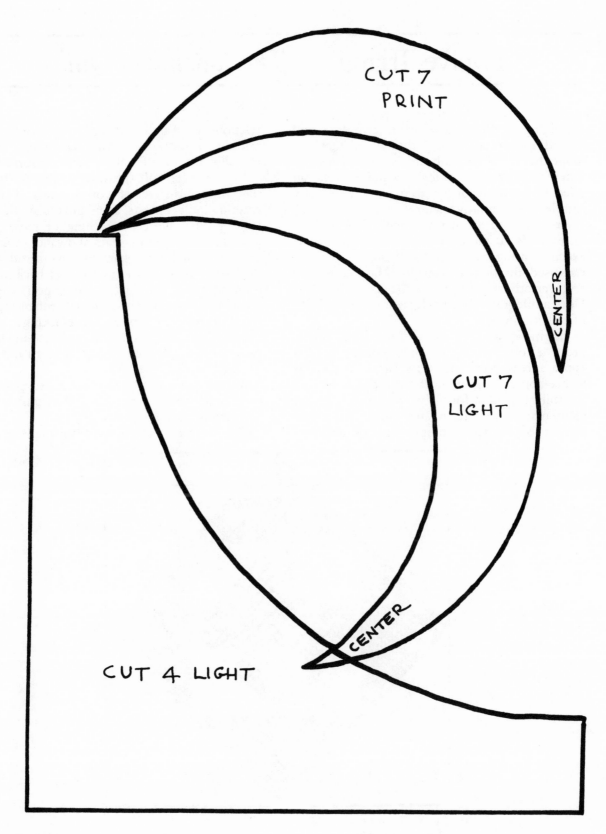

Naomi's Pinwheel
12-inch block
A trial block is in order to test skill, correctness of pattern
transfer, and seam allowance.

Twelve Triangles: *The Judging of Quilts*

Judging a quilt show is an awesome and unsettling responsibility. Although I sometimes judge them, I prefer quilt shows without awards where there are no hurt feelings and viewers can select their own favorites. To me, no matter how simple, every quilt is a winner.

Any kind of art work is judged on certain criteria. Is a piece well-planned and well-executed using quality craftsmanship? Do materials used suit the artist's purpose? Does the work reveal creativity, sensitivity, and mastery of form? Does it integrate all these elements into an object of esthetic appeal?

Judging quilts calls for additional guidelines. From a total of one hundred points, general appearance is worth ten points. I look for quality-of-eye appeal, condition of surface and over-all suitability. I allot forty-five points for design elements: composition and color, appropriateness of borders, complement of quilting, relationship of light and dark tones, success as a traditional pattern or original work. Workmanship accounts for the remaining forty-five.

Most judges will spend the major portion of their time in the area of workmanship. If you are entering quilt contests, avoid pitfalls by watching these points: perfect matching of pieces; true grain line throughout; seam allowance pressed to one side; matching or harmonizing thread; appliqué work matched to grain line of background; no unsightly shadowing-through; no raw edges; set of blocks correctly matched; enhancing and framing borders; no visible markings; small, even quilting stitches; backing seamed in vertical panels, not at the center; edges smooth and well-finished, with good corners.

If you can comply with all these points of judgment, you will have first-class quilts in the prize-winning circle.

The Twelve Triangles quilt was made in Mur-

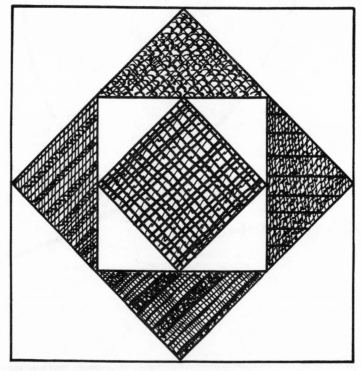

TWELVE TRIANGLES
Maker: unknown
Rutherford County, Tennessee, c. 1870
Black solid, striped, and print scraps combined with lighter-colored scraps and plain muslin; stripped in black with grey intersections.

freesboro, Tennessee, about 1870. I liked its sharp, clean design. Black solids, stripes, and print scraps combine with light fabric and muslin to give a strong image. Blocks were stripped in black with gray squares at the intersections. Quilt judges would have given the Twelve Triangles quilt a low mark because of its long, uneven quilting stitches of black thread in irregular concentric rows of fan quilting. Nevertheless, it is as dynamic as any op-art painting on a museum wall. (See color photographs for a close-up of the block and a view of the quilt.)

Twelve Triangles
9-inch block
Simplicity of design contributes to a dramatic quilt.

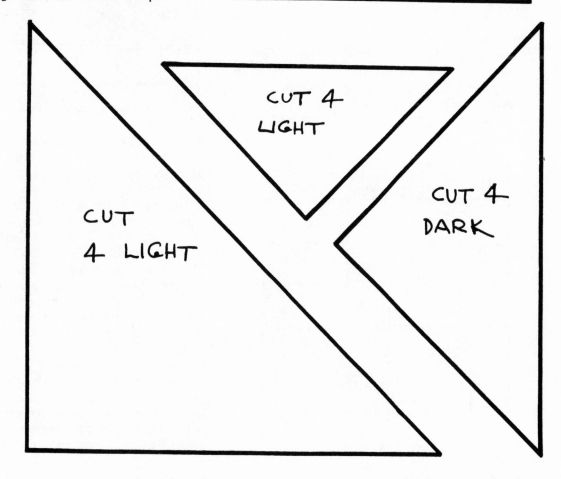

CUT 1
DARK
CENTER

CUT 4
LIGHT

CUT 4
DARK

CUT
4 LIGHT

SETTING THE QUILT BLOCKS

After the pleasant routine of sewing pieces into blocks has been completed, the task of "setting" them together deserves thoughtful study for there are so many different possibilities. I like to spread the blocks on a bed and try several arrangements, moving the blocks around until they seem comfortable, until I am satisfied. The room, the light, the height of the bed, the period of the furniture, the color of the walls, and the accessories in the room all enter into the decisions you make. If the quilt is to be used as a spread, allowance must be made for the turn up over the pillows and sufficient length on the sides.

Before assembly begins, check the blocks to be sure they are uniform in size; correcting any errors or discarding misfits at this point makes it easier to form even rows with your blocks later. Next press the blocks, turning the seams away from lighter pieces. A dark seam showing through a light piece is unattractive.

Consider these possibilities for assembling your blocks.

Block to Block

Sewing one block to another in rows of desired length and then joining the rows together to complete the top is the simplest plan. When blocks are placed next to each other, a pattern like the Nine Patch becomes an all-over pattern of regular squares. With planned organization of color, a definite design will emerge. The easiest of patterns can be as visually rewarding as one that is complicated.

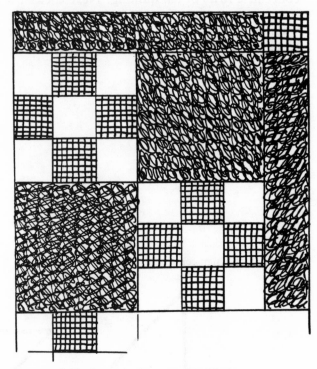

Nine Patch blocks with alternate plain blocks

Pieced and Unpieced Alternating Blocks.

Assume you are setting a Nine Patch. You may alternate a pieced block with an unpieced block of the same size. Success depends upon the selection of the material for your alternate blocks and how pleasingly you arrange plain and patterned, as well as light and dark for balance and contrast. Achieve an old-fashioned look by using a dark, small-floral print for the alternate blocks and border. The alternate plain block may be used for fancy quilting or even for stuffing. Originality, innovation, and invention are highly desirable. Their main ingredients are time and thought.

Stripped or Sashed Blocks

The Nine Patch or any other block can be joined by stripping it with one or more pieces of fabric to make a pronounced grid pattern on the quilt. The strip size is a matter of choice, varying usually from two inches to four inches. Needless

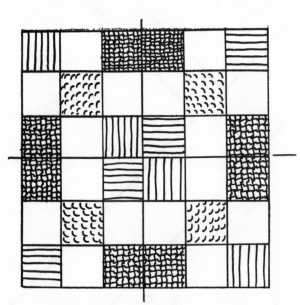

Four Nine Patch blocks joined together

to say, corners and rows must match both vertically and horizontally. Be careful to select stripping that is harmonious with the blocks, for if the strips are in too strong a color, they will dominate the blocks and make an overpowering grid. If the color is lighter than the main color of the block or pleasantly figured, the result should be satisfying.

Stripping may consist of a single piece of fabric or be as elaborate as a wide strip banded on either side by contrasting material. Intersections deserve special treatment, especially when the triple band is used. Perhaps a square of another color

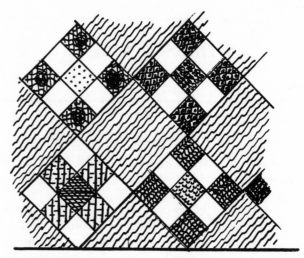

Diagonal set

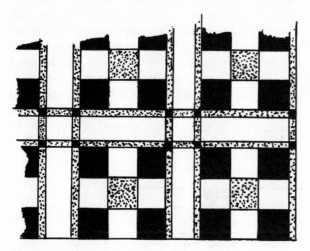

Triple stripping

can be set there, or a small, pieced block like the Pinwheel, Four Square or Nine Patch. Give the outer edge of the quilt a row or two of stripping to make a border.

Diagonal Blocks

Blocks become more dramatic when placed in a diagonal setting, or "on point." Try them on the bed and see what a difference half a turn makes. Any of the previous layouts may be used. Instead of placing the squares parallel to the sides of the bed, put them on the diagonal. Use stripping or alternate plain blocks or neither. Remember that the triangles forming the sides must be given an outer seam allowance; they are not made by cutting squares in half! A border, perhaps four inches wide, will provide the necessary frame for your work.

Alternating Blocks of Two Patterns

For a little adventure, see what happens when you alternate two different patterns of blocks. You might experiment with Nine Patch and Roman Stripe in equal size. You may come up with something new or re-invent an old favorite. This is a good exercise to try out on graph paper.

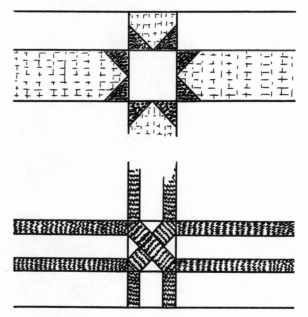

Intersection patterns

As you can see by these examples, the Nine Patch and any other properly nurtured block can become a quilt of refinement and beauty. These suggestions, along with your own variations, should help you plan the setting of your next quilt.

Tennessee Circles: *Commemoration of the 1982 World's Fair*

❖

Barbara Brackman described seventeen bright and lively patterns in an article celebrating the Knoxville World's Fair for the May 1982 issue of *Quilter's Newsletter Magazine*.

Tennessee Circles is an unusual block-to-block arrangement that makes a beautifully flowing and moving design, although it may not be apparent when you look at a single block. The image can be seen by drawing repeat blocks on graph paper or making multiple copies on a copy machine and placing the blocks together or arranging them in different ways. When four Tennessee Circles blocks are put together, a circle will be formed by the curved edge of the crosses.

The diagonal direction of the crosses and the interplay of circles gives great vitality to the rectangular composition and makes a beautiful quilt.

Author Barbara Brackman included this fascinating design in her mammoth *Encyclopedia Of Pieced Quilt Patterns* wherein she identifies patterns by name, and also documents the known published sources of the patterns. The source of many quilt patterns is difficult to discover, because the patterns were invented, used, and exchanged for years before they were shown in publication. Others originated on the drawing board of a quilt-column writer or pattern de-

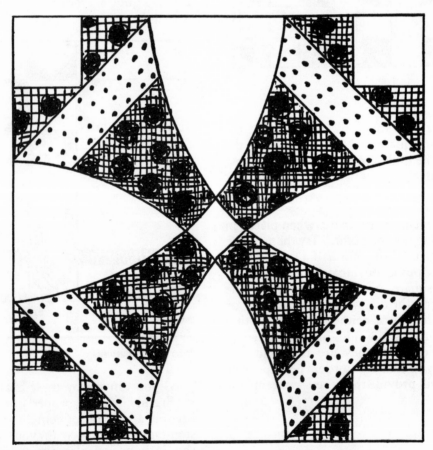

TENNESSEE CIRCLES
A quilt for any season and year.

signer. Ms. Brackman does her best to track them down. To compound the task, some patterns have multiple names. The Tennessee Snowball, for instance, can be called Flagstone, Improved Nine Patch, Mystery Snowball, Federal Chain, Aunt Patty's Favorite, Aunt Patsy's Pet, Four and Nine Patch, The Snowball and Nine Patch, Grandmother Short's Quilt.

Since curves require more patience, it would be best to try a sample block before committing yourself to a long-term project with the Tennessee Circles design.

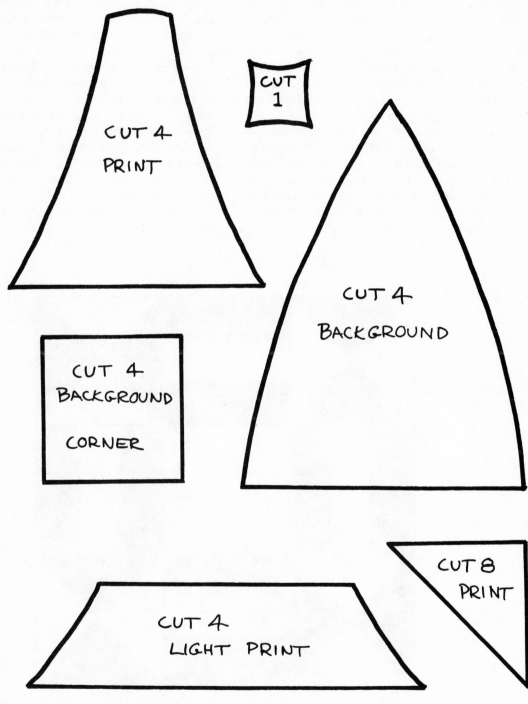

Tennessee Circles
9-inch block
As with many patterns, Tennessee Circles lends itself to scrap piecing when each square is made of different materials.

London Roads: *A Heritage Pattern*

❖

A Knoxville group, the Thursday Bee of the Smoky Mountain Quilters, made a heritage quilt as part of the celebration of Tennessee quiltmaking. Many of them had helped with Quilt Days and enjoyed the discovery of patterns new to them as they watched the quilts go by. As they saw more and more quilts they were challenged to recreate some of the designs. The Tennessee Heritage Quilt gradually evolved.

Linda Claussen made the first reproduction block and chose as her model an intricate pieced quilt, Friendship, which belongs to the Newport-Cocke County Museum in Newport, Tennessee. The results were gratifying; others decided to follow her example. Makers of the Tennessee Heritage Quilt practiced copying and drafting

patterns while they learned about nineteenth century dyeing and quiltmaking. Eva Earle Kent lent her expert help whenever needed.

Another member copied the London Roads pattern in Turkey-red and grey-blue fabric. Nancy Henrietta Denny made the original quilt about 1900 at her home in the Buffalo Valley area of Tennessee, and it was quilted at a quilting bee. Its maker was an expert needlewoman who enjoyed teaching the craft to her many grandchildren. She made everyday quilts from simple designs in practical colors which wouldn't show the soil and reserved fancier patterns and light colors for "company" quilts.

To make the project authentic, the group elected to use natural-dyed fabric typical of the

LONDON ROADS: A Tennessee Heritage Pattern
Maker: Nancy Henrietta Carlen Denny
Buffalo Valley, Tennessee, c. 1900
Blue print and green print cotton fabric set with red.

nineteenth century. Dr. James Liles, Professor of Zoology at the University of Tennessee, Knoxville, supplied cloth dyed according to processes used before the advent of synthetic dyes. One of Jim's specialties has been the study of Turkey-red dye which produces a deep, rich color. His Turkey-red is included in the quilt along with more subtle shades from the dye-pot. The cotton batt was hand-carded by Dale Liles.

Rather than plan uniform-sized blocks, the group made its heritage quilt blocks any size whatever and joined them in block-to-block fashion making a gigantic puzzle. Precedent for this arrangement came from a top made about 1870 by Iora Philo Pool of Sunbright, Tennessee, now owned by her great-granddaughters, Betty Holman Pickett and Gwen Holman Kelly.

You will find the London Roads block among the many stitched together to make this heritage quilt in the colored photographs section of this book.

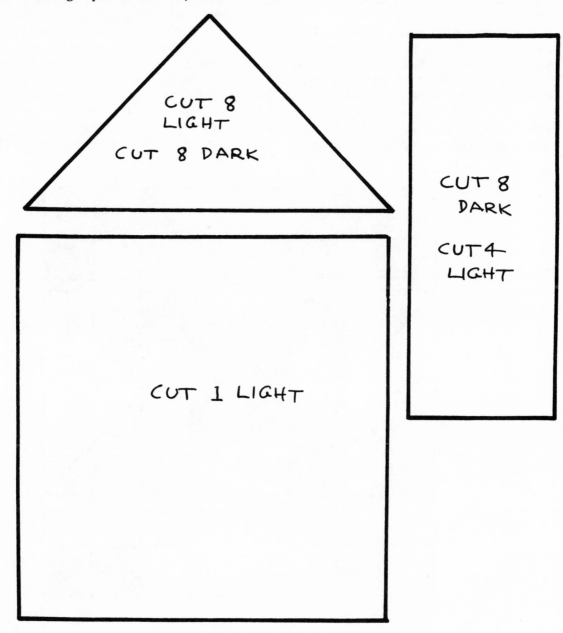

London Roads
12-inch block
A good pattern for scrap piecing by making each block of different material and setting the blocks together with sashing.

Ora's Crosspatch: *Diagonally Set Blocks*

As with any hobby, quilt-pattern collecting can be a full-time job. Once you are hooked, you will spend hours searching, cataloguing, filing, corresponding, developing cross-references, and so on. Some of my friends, experts in the field, have come to my aid when I needed help with identification.

When I find a design new to me, I look through my reference books to find it—sometimes an easy task, sometimes not. A block can look completely different when color and value changes are made or when the position is not the same, so I have seldom been brave enough to say I have discovered a new pattern. I let experts decide if it is a previously-unpublished design. Then,

publishing our discoveries makes more patterns available to quiltmakers.

Ora Humberd has an unnamed quilt set together about 1900 from pieces given to her mother, Eula Parris Smith, by Sis Parris Warren who was leaving Pickett County, Tennessee, to move to Texas. Small squares and triangles are set diagonally and alternated with rose-colored calico blocks to make a crisp, clear design with a great deal of style.

I searched and found nothing like it in my books, so I named it Ora's Crosspatch. The pattern lends itself to scrap-piecing with the smallest of scraps for the 1½-inch squares, and even more diminutive triangles. Blocks can be set

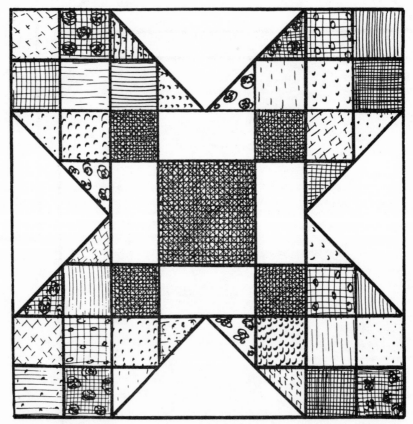

ORA'S CROSSPATCH
Maker: Sis Parris Warren and Eula Parris Smith
Pickett and Overton Counties, Tennessee, c. 1900
Colorful scraps surround a Nine Patch center that is made of the same material throughout. Set on the diagonal with alternate squares of rose calico.

[*Plate A*] LONE STAR. Maker: Glennie Mantooth, Newport, Tennessee, 1933.

[*Plate B*] MINIATURE EIGHT-POINTED STAR. Maker: Emma Woods, Middle Tennessee, 1880.

[*Plate C*] SWING IN THE CENTER. Maker: Lois Hall, Vonore, Tennessee, c. 1940.

[*Plate D*] LITTLE BRITCHES. Makers: Susie Drucilla Greer Cope and Addie Lee Cope Butler, Henry County, Tennessee, 1920.

[*Plate E*] APPALACHIAN SPRING. Designer and maker: the author, assisted by Lillie Johnson and June Miller, Chattanooga, Tennessee, 1983.

[*Plate F*] ROSE APPLIQUÉ. Maker: Cecella George Grubb of East Tennessee, c. 1870.

[*Plate G*] COCKSCOMB AND CURRANTS. Maker: Lizzie Nelson Burks, Rutherford County, Tennessee, c. 1890.

[*Plate H*] TENNESSEE HERITAGE QUILT. Maker: The Thursday Bee of the Smoky Mountain Quilters, Knoxville, Tennessee, 1987.

[Plate I] STRING-PIECED EIGHT-POINTED STAR. Maker: unknown, Jonesborough, Tennessee, c. 1890.

[Plate J] LONE STAR WITH SWAG BORDER. Maker: Martha Seacord, possibly Chattanooga, Tennessee, c. 1870—1880.

[Plate K] SOUTHERN CHARM. Designer and maker: the author, Chattanooga, Tennessee, 1987.

[Plate L] PINWHEEL. Maker: great-grandmother of Thelma Bacon Swafford, McMinn County, Tennessee, c. 1850.

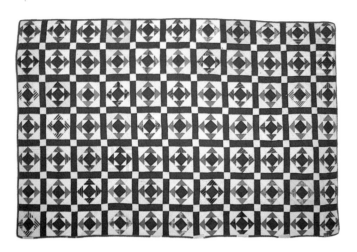

[*Plate M*] TWELVE TRIANGLES. Maker: unknown, Middle Tennessee, c. 1890.

[*Plate N*] TWELVE TRIANGLES. Close-up view.

[*Plate O*] BOWTIE. Maker: Jemima Lamon, Pigeon Forge, Tennessee, 1910–1920.

[*Plate P*] ORA'S CROSSPATCH. Makers: Sis Parris Warren and Eula Parris Smith, Pickett and Overton counties, Tennessee, c. 1900.

together with stripping or alternated with plain blocks like Ora's; I prefer an allover design of block set to block. The center nine patches can be made of the same material throughout the quilt to give a measure of unity.

Piece in units: the corner four patch, the center nine patch, and the side piece with the large triangle. Then assemble.

A colored photograph of Ora's Crosspatch appears in this book.

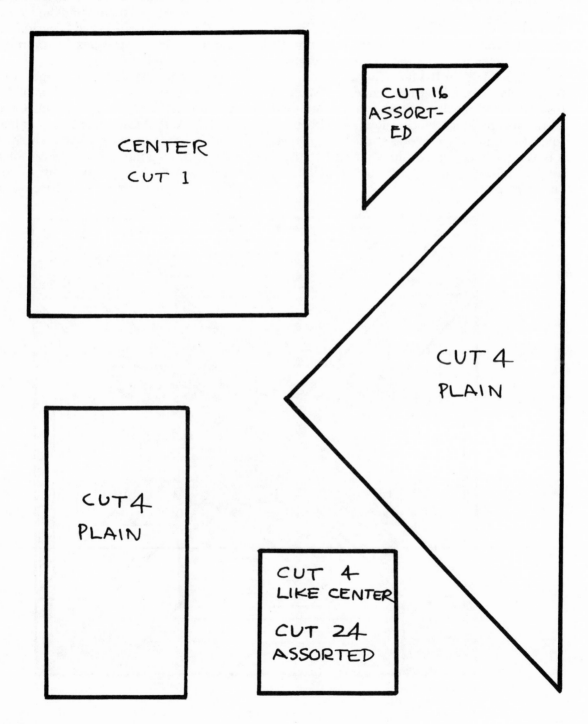

CENTER
CUT 1

CUT 16 ASSORTED

CUT 4 PLAIN

CUT 4 PLAIN

CUT 4 LIKE CENTER

CUT 24 ASSORTED

Ora's Crosspatch
12-inch block
A charming mixture of colorful print fabrics.

Tennessee Star: *A Mystery Pattern*

Appliqué quilts, by their very nature, are less standardized than pieced quilts and are often difficult to trace to their origins. Pieced quilts generally follow standard forms that can be found in reference books. The Tennessee Star, made about 1850 in Bradley County, belongs to Nancy Martin of Cleveland, Tennessee. Made of rose calico, with yellow-orange, and white solid fabric, its appliquéd blocks alternate with plain squares of pink rosebuds on a white background. It is a clear-cut design I could not locate in any of my reference books, hence the appellation, "mystery pattern."

Many Southern quiltmakers favor star patterns for their work. So many kinds and varieties exist that a complete book could be written about star patterns. (See illustrations for more star variations on the following pages.)

Timexenia M. Morris Roper of Stewart County, Tennessee, made a Star of Bethlehem quilt for her son, Emmett Allan Roper, during the Civil War. Around the points of her star, she filled in the area with three-inch squares containing eight-pointed stars instead of the more usual plain pieces. To give a lift of color, Mrs. Roper dyed her husband's tobacco sacks bright

TENNESSEE STAR
Maker: unknown
Bradley County, Tennessee, c. 1850
Blocks made of rose calico, yellow-orange and white solid cotton fabric alternating with squares of pink rosebuds on white background.

yellow-orange and mixed pieces of them in with her other scraps. She made a stunning quilt for her son and his son was proud to inherit the quilt from him.

Emma Woods of Middle Tennessee made a quilt of the LeMoyne Star design about 1880, but she used 2-inch squares of eight-pointed stars—an incredible feat of piecing. It is unlikely that readers will want to undertake a similar project—sewing tiny bits of cloth together to make 750 star blocks for a quilt top. The quilt is now owned by Dot Davis of Hixson, Tennessee. (Mrs. Woods' quilt and several other star quilt designs appear among the colored photographs).

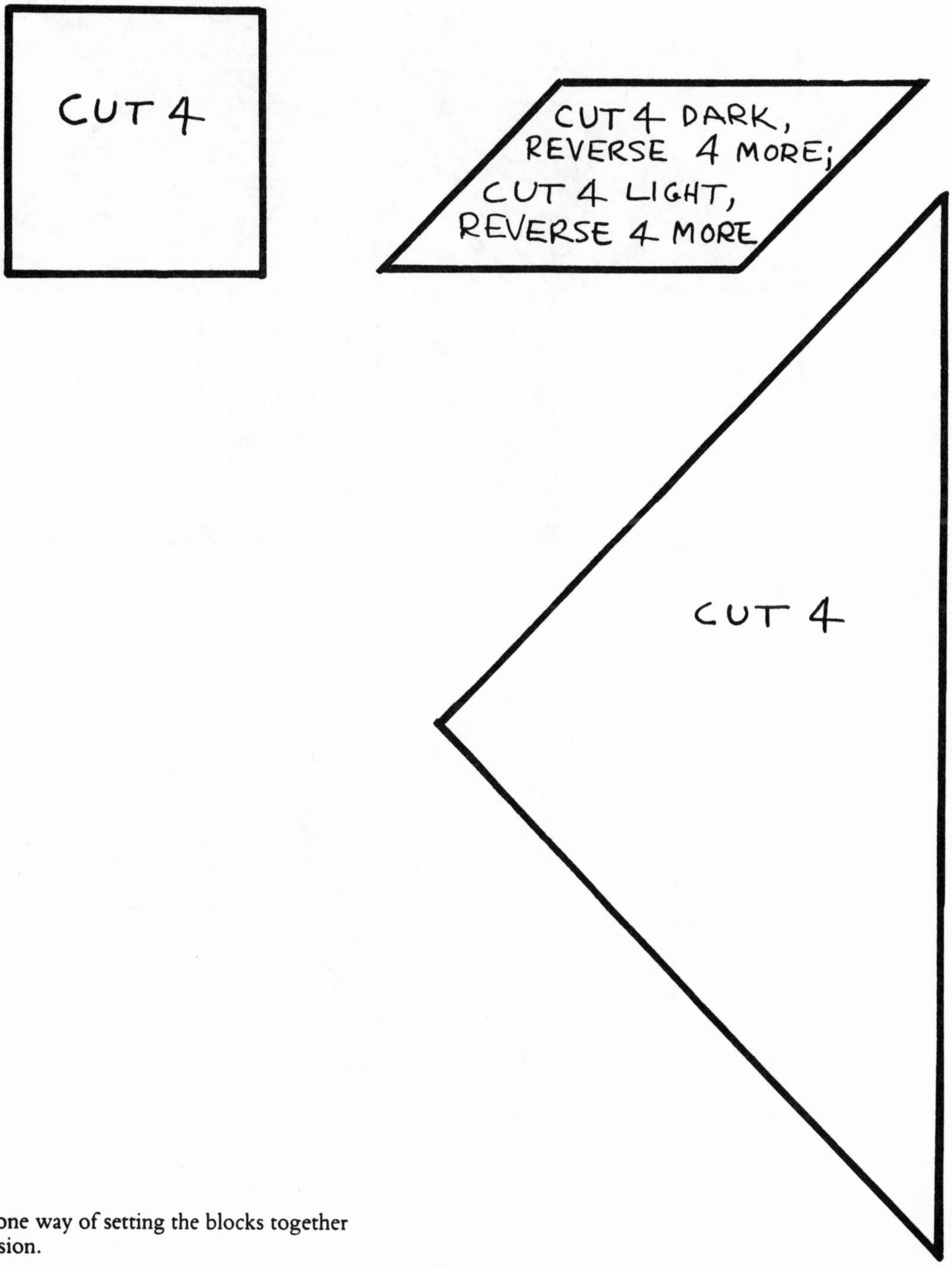

CUT 4

CUT 4 DARK,
REVERSE 4 MORE;
CUT 4 LIGHT,
REVERSE 4 MORE

CUT 4

Tennessee Star
9-inch block
Consider more than one way of setting the blocks together before making a decision.

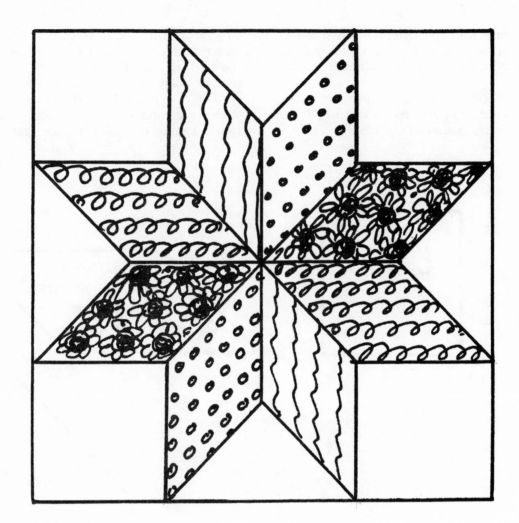

LeMoyne Star

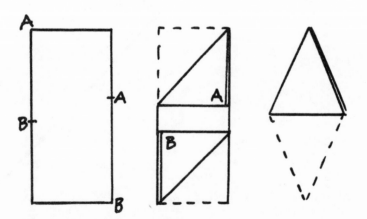

How to fold a dollar bill into a diamond

The Star of Heaven
6-inch block for center medallion of crib quilt designed by
Linda Claussen
Manger may be pieced (A, B, and C) or appliquéd onto D,
omitting C. Appliqué semi-circles to D and join top half to
lower half of square.

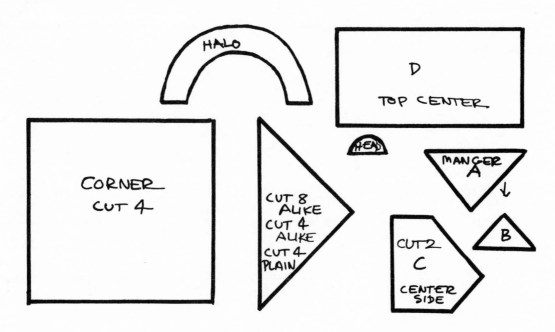

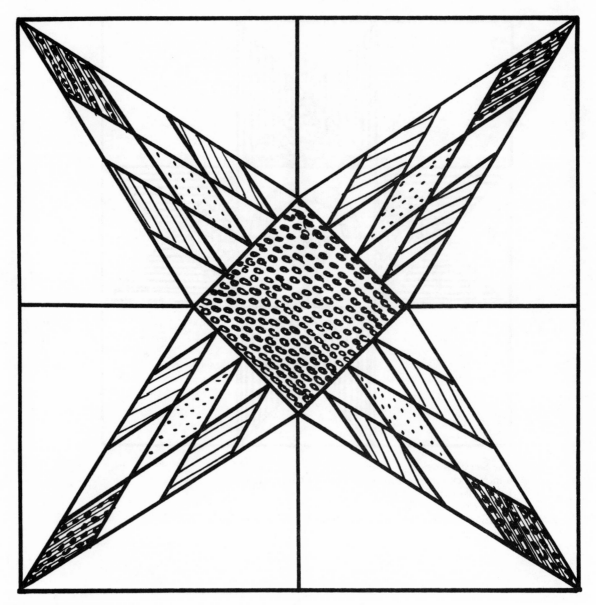

Four-Pointed Star

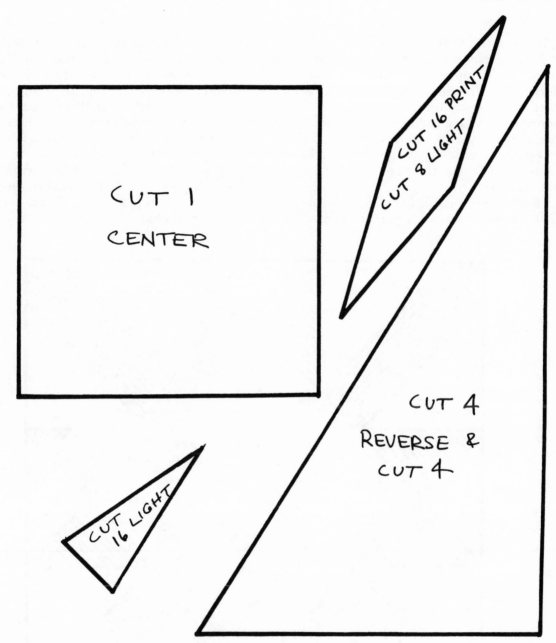

CUT 1

CENTER

CUT 16 PRINT

CUT 8 LIGHT

CUT 4

REVERSE &

CUT 4

CUT 16 LIGHT

Four-Pointed Star, a twelve-inch block

Tennessee Crossroads: *Four Ts for Tennessee*

Tennessee is a long, narrow state. The beauty of the landscape and the changing terrain from Bristol to Memphis help make the journey a pleasant one. Traveling the distance today at high speed in relative comfort, we can appreciate what pioneers must have endured two hundred years ago. They crossed the state on horseback, by boat or wagon, or on foot; and the trip was long and dangerous. "To undertake a journey" was not an idle phrase.

I found a quilt-block pattern in the February 1930 issue of *Needlecraft,* a popular magazine for women at that time. Its design exemplifies the criss-crossing of country roads and highways before interstates became a part of our lives. A slightly different version, the Turnbout T, appeared in the December 1930 *Kansas City Star.*

This pattern lends itself to machine or hand-piecing. Use scraps or choose three fabrics. If the blocks are set together without stripping, a pleasant allover pattern will emerge. If your name begins with T, the four Ts, one at each corner of the block, could make this your monogram quilt.

TENNESSEE CROSSROADS: Four Ts for Tennessee
An old and favorite pattern.

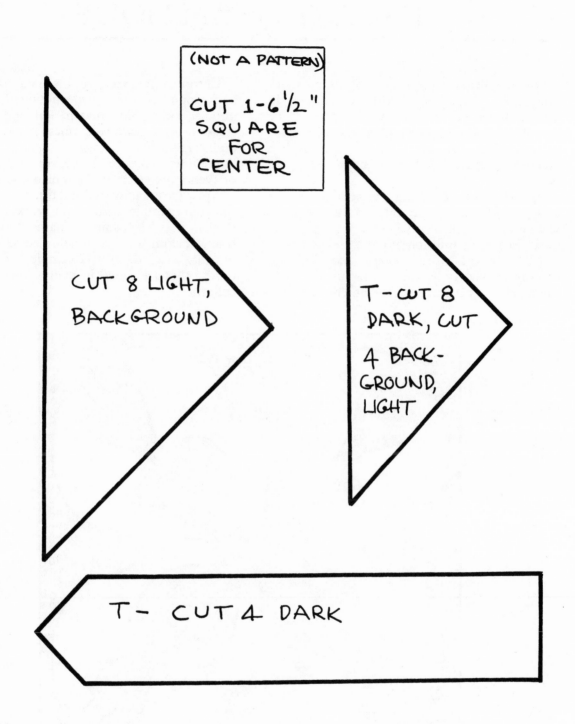

(NOT A PATTERN)

CUT 1-6 1/2"
SQUARE
FOR
CENTER

CUT 8 LIGHT,
BACKGROUND

T-CUT 8
DARK, CUT
4 BACK-
GROUND,
LIGHT

T- CUT 4 DARK

Tennessee Crossroads
12-inch block
For the center cut a 6½″ square. This includes ¼″ seam
allowance.

THE ART OF APPLIQUÉ

Some quiltmakers consider appliqué-work more difficult than pieced-work. I don't agree. In fact, I prefer to do appliqué because of the complete freedom in making the design. Pieced-work requires units which must fit together in a precise way and calls for a different type of design skill.

Appliqué means applying a piece of fabric to a background material. Because it is similar to sewing on a patch, it is sometimes called *patchwork*. To avoid confusion of terms, however, we usually use the word *appliqué* and *pieced* to describe the two types of quilts and use the word *patchwork* as a general term for either one.

Cutting out shapes and sewing them to a background block is easy enough if you have good scissors, some imagination, and an understanding of a few basic rules. Many styles of quilts are made in this way, ranging from simple Sunbonnet Babies to the elegant Rose of Sharon or even more elaborate Hawaiian quilts.

Appliqué is a universal and timeless art. *Molas,* splendid examples of appliqué work, come from the San Blas Islands near Panama. In Cambodia layers of cloth are cut and hemmed back to make intricate maze designs. Examples of these and other types are found in many museum textile collections.

HEARTS
Designer: the author
Chattanooga, Tennessee, 1981
A cutout of red print fabric applied to white cotton background.

Wholecloth appliqué as practiced in Hawaii is somewhat different. A design is frequently stylized from a botanical subject, cut by pattern from a large single or seamed piece of cloth and basted to the background material. It takes many hours to complete the sewing and quilting. Traditionally, each quilter makes her own design.

The same method can be used to make original designs for smaller projects. You may remember cutting out snowflakes from folded paper. Instead of the lacy delicacy of snowflakes, try simpler shapes when you plan to work with fabrics. Fold a very thin paper, like tissue paper, in quarters (two folds), sixths (in half, then in thirds), or eighths. Try several designs until you get one you like that is suitable for appliqué. Your new design can be used for a single block as a pillow or wall hanging or as the center medallion of a quilt. It can be repeated in blocks for a whole quilt, or it can be used with others in a sampler quilt.

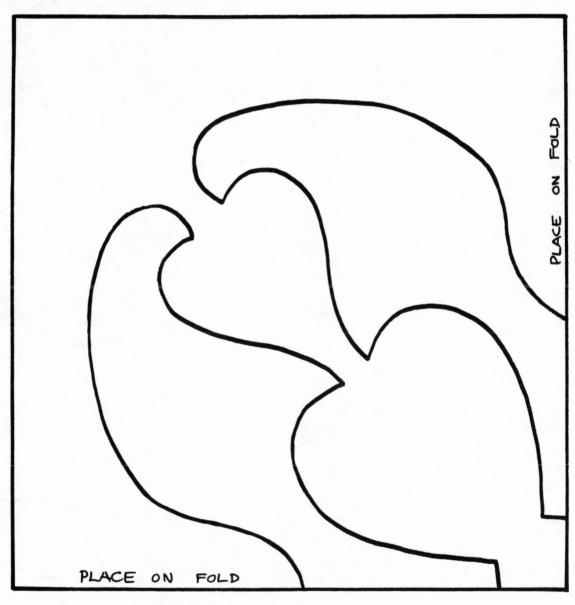

Hearts
12-inch block
One-fourth of the pattern is shown. To make a full pattern, place pattern on a square of paper folded into fourths. When cut from folded cloth, layers may be discrepant.

The Bridesmaid: *Hints for Appliqué*

Cotton cloth works best for appliqué. Synthetics do not turn under as well and have a tendency to ravel more. You need good cutting scissors, a pair of sharp embroidery scissors, thimble, fine needle of your choice (I prefer #8, #9, or #10 crewel needles), silk pins, and sewing thread, preferably cotton.

Wash and iron all material to remove sizing and insure that one material will not shrink more than another when the finished work is washed. Remove the selvages. Work with the grain of the material, matching applied pieces to the grain of the background material. When cutting a piece by a pattern, place pattern on background in the desired position and mark the straight of the goods. Cut the piece out accordingly. You may prefer to cut directly from the cloth without a pattern, trying to match the grain the same way. (Quilt judges look for that sort of thing.)

Pin pieces in position. Large pieces may need some center vertical and horizontal basting. Do not baste or press under the edge. You want the edges to respond to the background material and rest comfortably against it. Pressing or turning and basting an edge will not make as subtle and flowing a line as when you let the applied piece have its way. Use as small a seam allowance as possible—about ³⁄₁₆-inch, but some fabric may require a little more.

Now you are ready to sew. Generally you will want to use thread matching the piece to be applied so your stitches show as little as possible. Sometimes you may choose a contrasting thread for accent or emphasis. Texture of thread is a matter of choice, also.

Start with a backstitch or single quilter's knot. Turn under the edge of the seam allowance with your finger or tip of the needle. I hold my work so the tucked edge is coming toward me or down with gravity. Some people prefer to tuck under the edge away from them. Use whichever way seems easiest for you. Turn the edge under for an inch or so as you hold it in place with the left thumb. It may be necessary to clip at corners and curved places, but do as little as possible. The edge will be smoother without it.

Use a blind-stitch, slip-stitch, whip-stitch, or even a running stitch. Sometimes an embroidery stitch may be effective. Use anything but a blanket-stitch in black thread; it looks ugly and will wear out before the rest of the thread and fabric.

Do not worry about corners until you get there. Sew all the way to the end of the stitching line. Trim away some of the excess at the point or corner if necessary. Then turn the point under, square across at right angles to the seam line. Tuck under the next portion of seam allowance. Take a couple of stitches at the point and proceed down the next side. Don't worry about what lies ahead, but do an inch at a time. End with back-stitches hidden under the edge or on the back of the foundation material.

THE BRIDESMAID
Designer: the author
Chattanooga, Tennessee, 1981
A collection of pastel dress fabrics, lace, and embroidery.

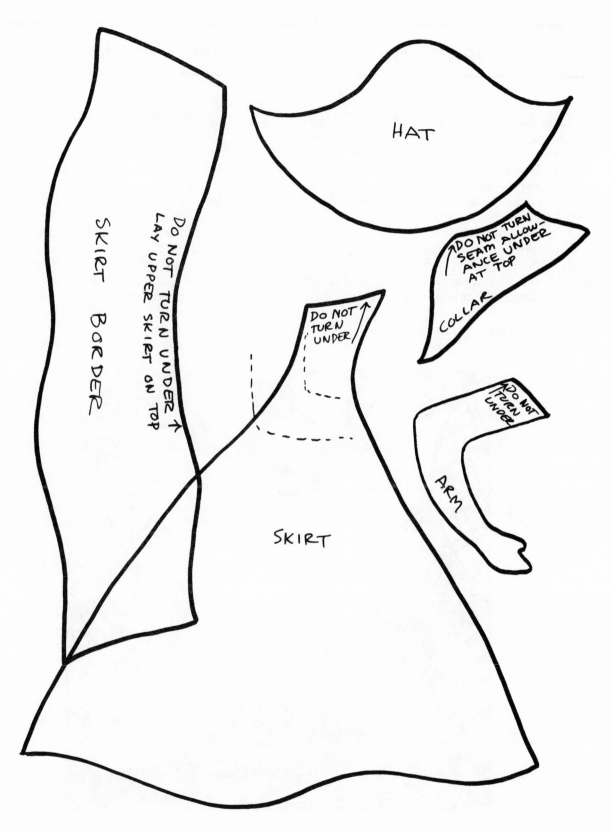

HAT

DO NOT TURN
SEAM ALLOW-
ANCE UNDER
AT TOP

COLLAR

SKIRT BORDER

DO NOT TURN UNDER →
LAY UPPER SKIRT ON TOP

DO NOT
TURN
UNDER ↑

DO NOT
TURN
UNDER

ARM

SKIRT

The Bridesmaid
9 x 12-inch foundation block
Another version of the Sunbonnet Baby, this one is for
young ladies.

Nameless Quilt: *A Simple Appliqué*

Quilts purchased or acquired as inheritance gifts seem like orphans unless they have a name. A quilt needs a name. Researchers are indebted to Barbara Brackman for *An Encyclopedia of Pieced Quilt Patterns,* an authoritative book whose entries come from newspapers, magazines, books, pattern books, and pamphlets.

Quite often people ask me to find the name of a quilt pattern and sometimes the answer comes easily. When it doesn't, the search begins. A friend needed help in identifying the block illustrated here. Its maker, now an elderly lady, had forgotten the name of the quilt she made about 1940 from a pattern in the Nashville *Tennessean*. The quilt uses predominantly blue

prints and solids, with some reds and a few other colors. Her block is a 10-inch square with assorted scraps appliquéd to it. The maker then joined the blocks without stripping. Perhaps someone who made this quilt or saved the newspaper clipping will volunteer the quilt's name, or a diligent researcher may wish to investigate further in the library's microfilm files of old newspapers.

To retain the name of your quilts, it's a good idea to add the quilt name when you sign and date the quilt. Marked antique quilts are far more valuable than those unmarked. Sign your new quilts, add the date, person for whom it was made, if relevant, and the pattern name.

NAMELESS QUILT
  Maker: unknown
  Nashville, Tennessee, c. 1940
  Assorted cotton scraps, mostly blue, applied to white foundation.

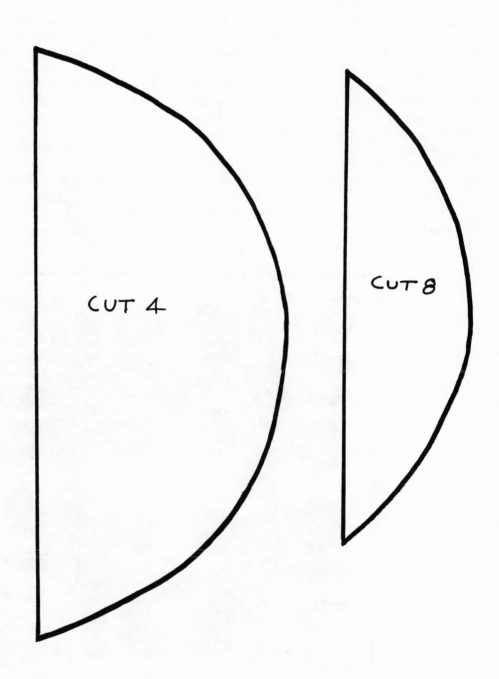

CUT 4

CUT 8

Nameless Quilt
10-inch foundation block
Add seam allowances to the block as well as to the pieces.
Join block to block.

Lobster Variation: *A Christmas Quilt*

Quiltmakers are kindly people. They think loving thoughts about their friends as they stitch. They care about their families and are fond of making gifts for them. They share patterns and fabric. A quilter is a good person to know.

If you are a maker of objects, you will probably want to make special gifts for Christmas and other occasions. I know of no better gift than a wall hanging or quilt, especially if it is done in seasonal colors.

Several of my friends have red and green quilts they save for Christmas. Spreading the quilt on a bed and hanging an everlasting pine-cone wreath on the wall decorates a room in an instant. I am sure families and friends remember the warmth of that room whenever they recall past years spent there.

Almost any quilt pattern, pieced or appliqué, can be used for a Christmas quilt. Red and green seem the obvious colors, but some people choose gold and white, silver and pink, or aqua, silver, and white as their themes for decorating. Whatever the pattern, carry those colors throughout the house.

I fell heir to a bold red and green appliquéd block made sometime in the late nineteenth century. It looks somewhat like Marguerite Ickis's The Lobster from *The Standard Book of Quilt Making,* although my design adds three pineapple-crown-shaped leaves at each corner—a wonderful, vibrant pattern, predominantly red, with green corners. The design would make a

LOBSTER VARIATION
Maker: unknown
Possibly Chattanooga area, c. 1890
Christmas-red solid and green print fabrics on white cotton.

striking wall hanging with the blocks set on the diagonal and surrounded by dark green corners and a frame border.

Several other seasonal wall hangings—Hearts, Spring Flowers, Sailboats, and Autumn Leaves— can establish the decorating theme for each season. Make them for yourself or as a gift, giving one annually until the set is complete.

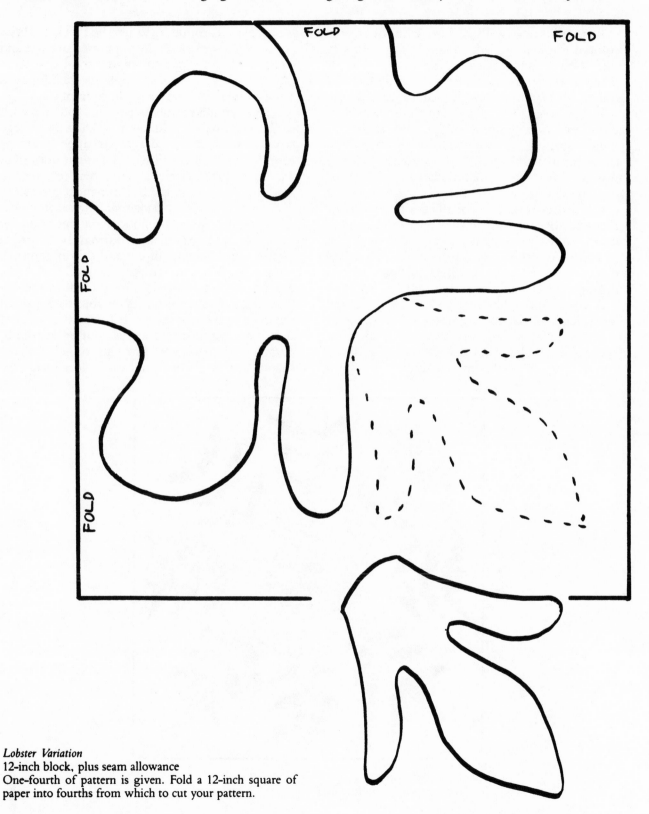

Lobster Variation
12-inch block, plus seam allowance
One-fourth of pattern is given. Fold a 12-inch square of paper into fourths from which to cut your pattern.

Rose of Tennessee: *From the Salad Bar*

❖

Rose quilts nearly always have white or cream-colored foundations which emphasize colors in their flowers and foliage. I do recall one quilt made in Baltimore about 1840 with pink calico squares between the appliquéd blocks. White spaces between the appliquéd sections were filled with elaborate quilting designs. In some instances stuffing was added to the quilted motifs from the underside of the quilt. Often homespun was used for the lining of such quilts perhaps from necessity, perhaps because threads could be conveniently separated for the stuffing process. Extra cotton was pushed through with a needle, thorn, quill, or ivory stiletto. On the reverse side of stuffed quilts you will usually be able to see places where extra cotton has been forced through the fabric.

A rose quilt is like a salad bar. Pick out the ingredients—flowers, buds, leaves—mix them together in a tasteful way, and put them on a background. The main flower can be built of several layers of petals and a center with buds and leaves placed around it. When the block has been constructed, the pieces are appliquéd in place and enough blocks repeated for the total quilt top. (An example of a rose appliqué can be seen among the book's colored photographs.)

I have supplied some shapes, but you may wish to make some of your own. Start with a large circular shape and add two or three layers or centers for the main flower. Then cut out leaves and buds of your choice and pin them in place. To appliqué, start with the bottom-most pieces.

A technique called *shadow quilting* is somewhat simpler than regular appliqué. First, cut a piece of background material approximately fourteen inches square, then a lining and thin batting the same size; layer the three pieces. Cut out the desired design, but do not include seam allowance. Arrange the pieces on your background material, and cover the entire top with a piece of sheer organza the same size as your background. Attach the organza with fine pins to anchor all the shapes in place. Then quilt each piece inside the

ROSE OF TENNESSEE
An old pattern thought to have originated in Tennessee.

edge and around the outside of the shape. Do more quilting to echo the shape or fill the background as you wish. Make a pillow back; add a ruffle, and you will have a lovely pillow.

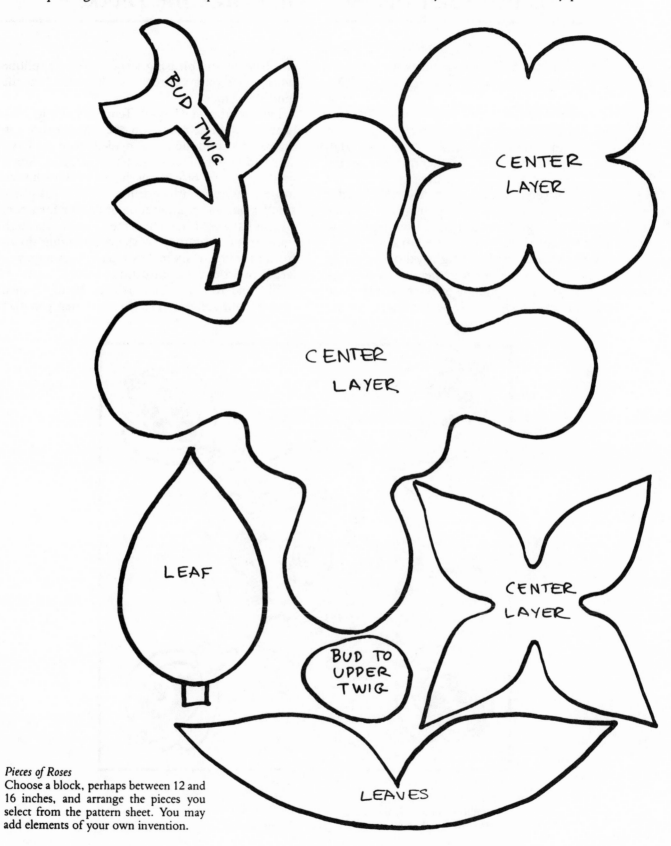

Pieces of Roses
Choose a block, perhaps between 12 and 16 inches, and arrange the pieces you select from the pattern sheet. You may add elements of your own invention.

Edith Hall's Rose: *What Size the Block?*

On occasion, people make quilt tops and store them away, planning to get to the quilting "sometime." During a ten-year stint as craft director for Senior Neighbors of Chattanooga, Inc., I saw an enormous variety of tops which our volunteers offered to quilt. Marjorie Hall brought in a top made by her mother in the 1920s, but it could well have been copied from a nineteenth-century quilt. She had appliquéd a Rose of Sharon with Pomegranates onto nine large blocks and framed them all with a narrow green border and a wider white border.

She set her deep rose, bright yellow, and pale green on white blocks together without stripping. A generous amount of white at the outer edges of each block gave good quilting space and emphasized the pleasing shapes of her appliqué work. The outer border's width added to the quilt's elegance.

During the survey of Tennessee quilts, we noticed a definite reduction of block size through the years. Appliqué quilts made before the Civil War had larger blocks and fewer of them. Some used only four blocks, perhaps thirty inches or more square, with borders added. Slightly smaller blocks required nine or twelve for a top. Blocks have continued to decrease in size through the twentieth century. With sizes ranging down from fourteen to six inches square, tops require a larger number for completion.

We tend to think of blocks as 10 to 15-inch squares, but consider a larger size when you plan

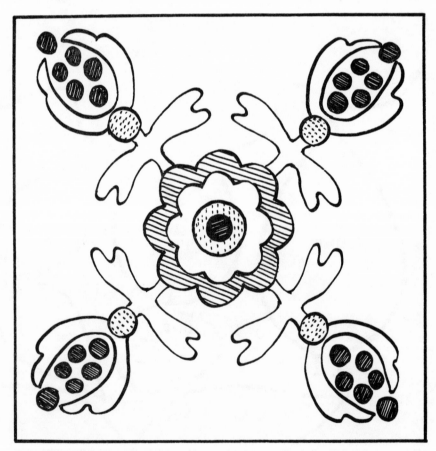

EDITH HALL'S ROSE
   Maker: Edith Lenis Fitzgerald Hall
   Hamilton County, Tennessee, c. 1920
   Deep rose, bright yellow, and pale green on white cotton.

an appliqué quilt. Nine 20-inch blocks will cover the top of a double bed; borders—plain, pieced, or appliquéd—make the overhang. A larger, bolder design will be much more dramatic than the multiple repetition of small blocks. By making large blocks you will be following an old tradition of southern quiltmaking.

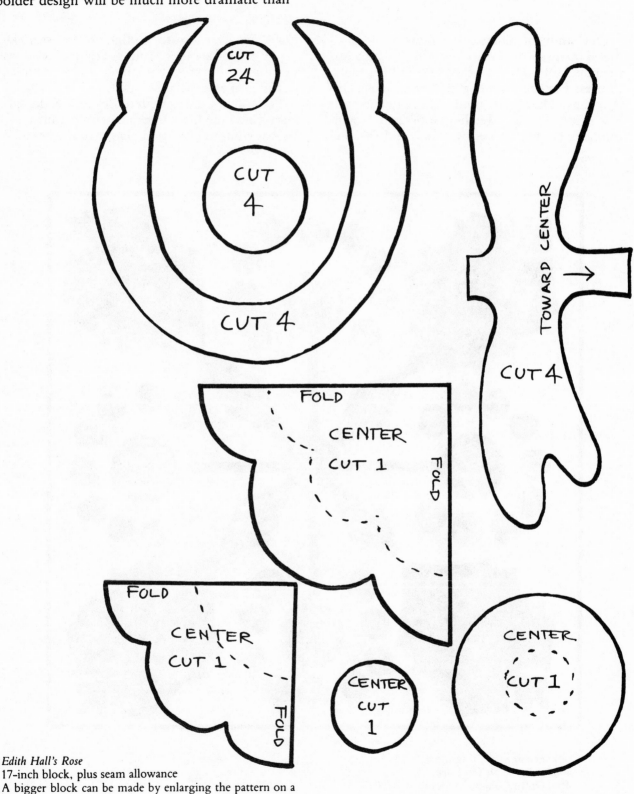

Edith Hall's Rose
17-inch block, plus seam allowance
A bigger block can be made by enlarging the pattern on a copy machine.

Cockscomb and Currants: *A Masterpiece Quilt*

Our study of nineteenth-century quilts produced many surprises, not the least of which was the popularity of the Cockscomb and Currants, Princess Feather, Plume, and their various combinations. They were produced as often in their day as the Double Wedding Ring and Grandmother's Flower Garden were in the 1930s and 1940s. We were amused to find ourselves thinking "Oh, not another Princess Feather!" even as we admired the precise stitching, and sometimes stuffing, of a masterpiece quilt.

These quilts, along with those of floral design, represented the highest refinement in quilt art—almost without exception. They required expen-

COCKSCOMB AND CURRANTS
Maker: Lizzie Nelson Burks
Rutherford County, Tennessee, c. 1890
Red and green solid colors on white cotton.

diture for materials after careful planning and were sewn with care, unhurriedly. Some of the quilts predate the Civil War, while others were made as late as 1910. It is possible that some of the late ones were copies of family heirlooms made from patterns passed down through several generations.

One of my favorite Cockscomb and Currants quilts was made by Lizzie Nelson Burks about 1890. She appliquéd nine blocks using the customary red and green fabric and put a swag border on one side (because only one side of the quilt would show on the bed). Her quilt, a wedding present for her son, won first prize in a Waco, Texas, fair in 1910. (A colored photograph of her quilt appears in this book.)

Even more spectacular is a quilt of Plumes and Roses made by Mary Newman Wattenburger in McMinn County, Tennessee, about 1910. The four large blocks and the overall style are much more typical of an earlier period. The quiltmaker added a more modern touch by appliquéing the vine border with the sewing machine.

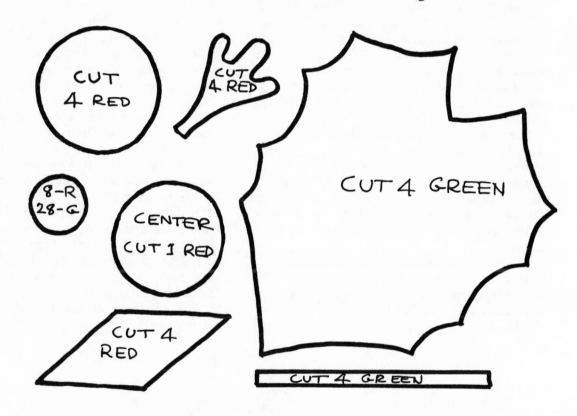

Cockscomb and Currants
12-inch square or larger, plus seam allowance
A true test of patience, but the results will be worth the trouble.

Dutch Tulip: *A Tale about Mildred Locke*

Nothing can destroy a lecturer more quickly than discovering she has the wrong set of slides in her carrying case. Mildred Locke, that composed and usually well-organized lady from Bell Buckle, Tennessee, did just that when we were invited to lecture at the Kentucky Heritage Quilt Society one year. We were expecting to hear about Grace Snyder, a renowned Nebraska quiltmaker, but instead we were treated to "Mildred Locke." Mildred did an on-the-spot autobiography because she did not have the right set of slides. It was a delightful experience, and I was glad for her mistake but sorry for her anguish.

She told the audience how early in her career as a quilting instructor she had stayed with my mother while attending the Southern Quilt Symposium. She told my mother that quiltmaking was becoming almost an obsession. Mildred said she felt guilty about spending so much time with quilts when other things were being neglected.

My mother assured Mildred she was being a missionary and doing good in the world by teaching people to do something satisfying. That apparently dispelled Mildred's guilt feeling, for she has been "doing good" ever since. She has experienced the satisfaction of knowing that each woman she teaches is able to find something to suit her individual interests. Each woman learns patience, care, and the art of selection. She finds the work soothing and peaceful—a help with worries and cares.

Mildred says that a woman's quilt is special in a way that no other thing is. It is a part of her eyes, her mind, her heart, and her endurance. It is, in truth, a part of its maker. Mildred Locke draws out each person she works with and challenges her to do her best.

"Your quilt is an opinion of yourself," she says.

Mildred Locke gives so much of herself to her work, and she never lets a challenge go by. When she had an opportunity to lure the National Quilting Association to Tennessee in 1983 for its annual meeting and exhibition, she put Bell Buckle on the map.

The Dutch Tulip block illustrated here is from a quilt Mildred owns. I first noticed it in an exhibition because it had been skillfully appliquéd with a treadle sewing machine. When it was hung for photographing during the survey of Tennessee quilts, the beauty of its over-all design became apparent. It has brought pleasure to many viewers since that day.

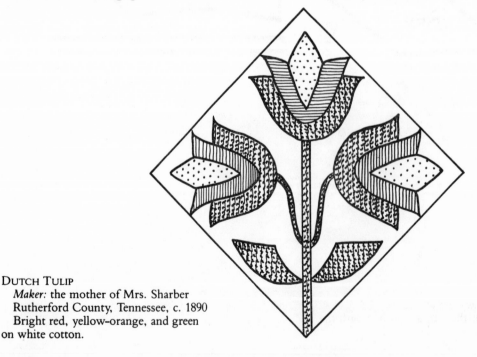

DUTCH TULIP
Maker: the mother of Mrs. Sharber
Rutherford County, Tennessee, c. 1890
Bright red, yellow-orange, and green
on white cotton.

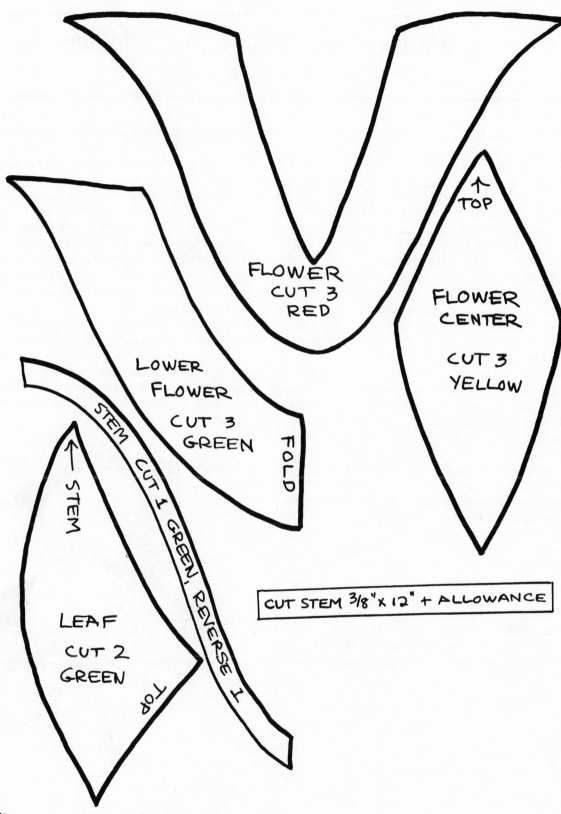

FLOWER
CUT 3
RED

↑
TOP

FLOWER
CENTER

CUT 3
YELLOW

LOWER
FLOWER

CUT 3
GREEN

FOLD

STEM CUT 1 GREEN, REVERSE 1

← STEM

↑ STEM

CUT STEM 3/8" x 12" + ALLOWANCE

LEAF
CUT 2
GREEN

TOP

Dutch Tulip
14–inch block
The maker appliquéd her pieces to the background with a
treadle sewing machine, but hand-appliqué is equally
acceptable.

Wildflower Garden: *A Collection of Spring Beauties*

While cleaning out and disposing of an aunt's household goods, I came across a little yellow envelope among some papers and letters. On the front was written, "A little bouquet gathered in summer—1908." Inside was a pressed sprig of yellow flowers. On what occasion were the wildflowers picked by a still-single young woman several years before her marriage? Why were they saved? Three photographs taken a year later show two couples standing beside a lake in a small town a considerable distance from my aunt's home. The women's white dresses are long and full-skirted, with tight bodices and puffed sleeves, the men wear dark suits. It is a romantic picture and now a mystery.

Many little bouquets have been pressed in books and Bibles in times past. Years later, one can only guess at the gatherer's story, yet the flowers remain faithfully in place. Besides beauty and fragrance, flowers have always carried special meaning for those who give and receive them.

Spring is a beautiful time in the South. Redbud nudges winter away; azaleas and dogwood soon open their showy blossoms. Bluebells or Virginia cowslips are favorites of mine. Their nodding pink buds open to light blue flowers standing straight and tall. Their leaves are velvety green in contrast to the clear blue of the blossoms.

I have designed a collection of wildflower patterns that may be used in a variety of ways. You could put them on single 7-inch squares and join them for an allover pattern of assorted wildflowers, or you could make one large square, perhaps of fourteen inches, and repeat four units of a single flower, later joining those with other squares and other flowers. You might make a large center medallion of a basket of flowers and border it with the smaller blocks, adding other bands and borders as needed to complete the top. You could select one flower design and use it exclusively to make units that you will set between plain blocks and quilt elaborately. (A close-up of a wildflower border appears among the colored photographs in this book.)

You are the designer. You choose the method and arrangement. The same fabric can be used for each flower unit, but a mixture of fabrics will be more true to nature. In their native habitat, plants do not look identical because of different light conditions, different surroundings, and variety within the species.

Although these patterns are intended for quilts, they may be used in other ways. Try them on small items like jackets, skirts, aprons, bags. Maybe you have a skirt which seems a little tired, or one with a stain that won't come out. Put a dogwood spray over it. Add a blouse or shirt, a velveteen vest in harmonizing colors, and enjoy the compliments.

Appliqué and quilt some pillow tops. Add a matching ruffle and a quilted back when you make them up. If you want to save time, make several to have on hand for birthday, wedding, and graduation presents. You will want to make an inner pillow to be removed when the top is laundered.

Trillium

WILDFLOWER GARDEN
Designer: the author
Chattanooga, Tennessee, 1983
Assorted colors with green on white cotton background, blue borders; incorporated in border of a quilt, Appalachian Spring. Made with the assistance of Lillie Johnson and June Miller. See colored photographs for border section.

As for pillow stuffing, feathers are wonderful but difficult to work with. Kapok makes a soft, fluffy filler that lasts for years. Some of the polyester stuffing works well, but it tends to pack together in time and does not have the "live" feeling of a natural material. Nylon stockings make a heavy, uninviting filler to touch. A pillow should feel pleasant and provide comfort as well as beauty. Let yours be your best expression.

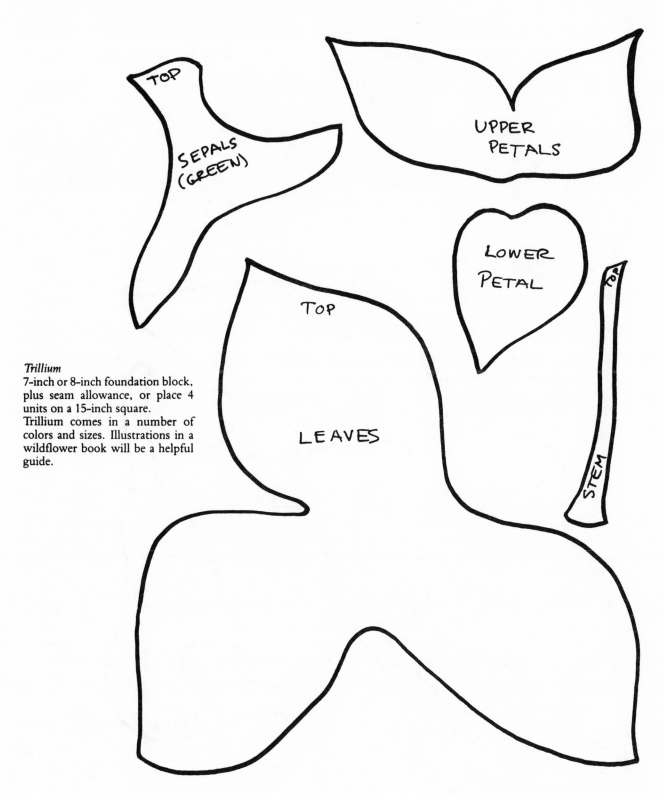

Trillium
7-inch or 8-inch foundation block, plus seam allowance, or place 4 units on a 15-inch square.
Trillium comes in a number of colors and sizes. Illustrations in a wildflower book will be a helpful guide.

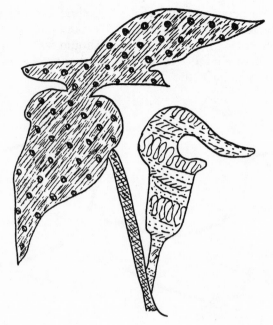

Jack-in-The-Pulpit
7-inch or 8-inch block
A reddish brown print serves well for the Jack.

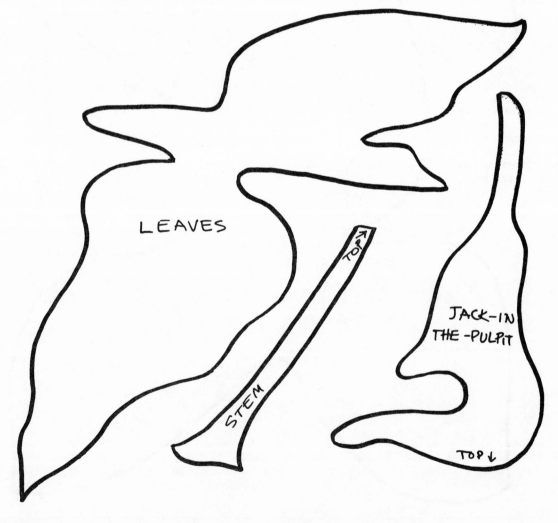

LEAVES

STEM

TOP

JACK-IN THE-PULPIT

TOP

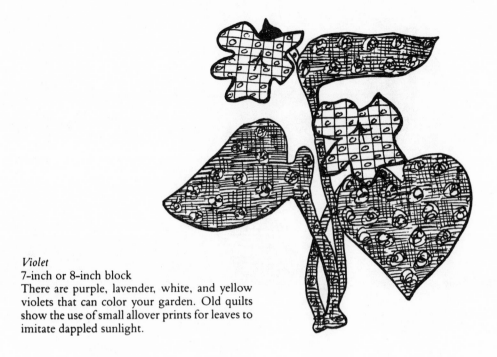

Violet
7-inch or 8-inch block
There are purple, lavender, white, and yellow violets that can color your garden. Old quilts show the use of small allover prints for leaves to imitate dappled sunlight.

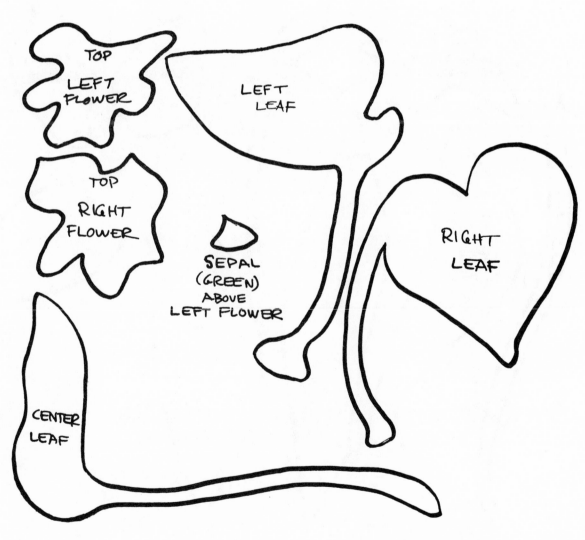

TOP LEFT FLOWER

LEFT LEAF

TOP RIGHT FLOWER

SEPAL (GREEN) ABOVE LEFT FLOWER

RIGHT LEAF

CENTER LEAF

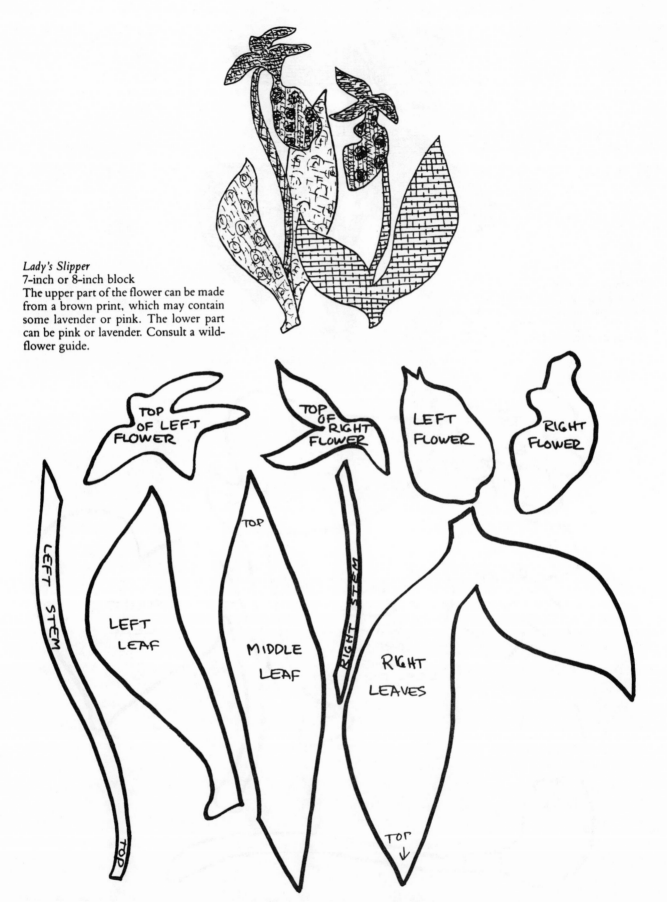

Lady's Slipper
7-inch or 8-inch block
The upper part of the flower can be made from a brown print, which may contain some lavender or pink. The lower part can be pink or lavender. Consult a wildflower guide.

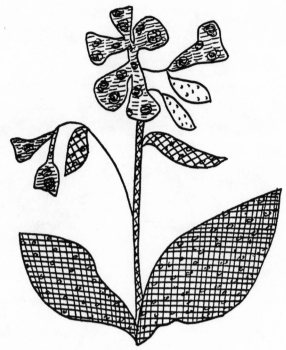

Bluebell
7-inch or 8-inch block
Bluebells are a clear, bright blue. Use pink for the two buds
on the right. Leaves are a rich green, shaded toward blue.

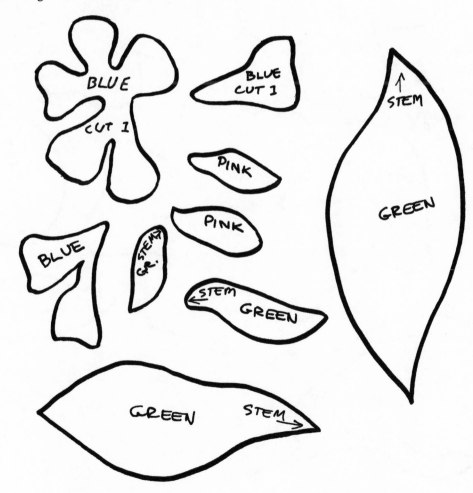

Dogwood
7-inch or 8-inch block
Blossoms can be made in a pale figured-and-white print or in pink. The leaves should not be too dark. Part of the stem can be embroidered.

Chart for placement of Dogwood pattern

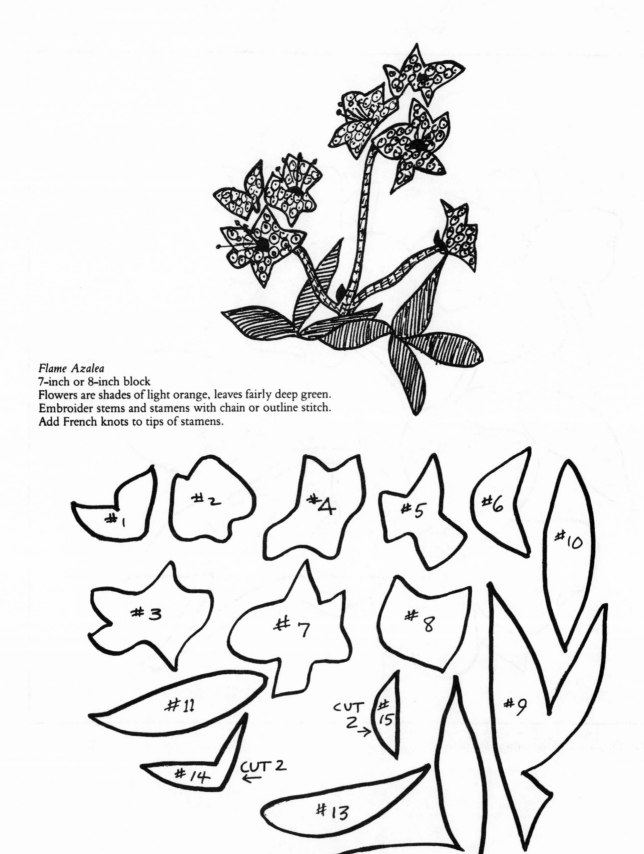

Flame Azalea
7-inch or 8-inch block
Flowers are shades of light orange, leaves fairly deep green.
Embroider stems and stamens with chain or outline stitch.
Add French knots to tips of stamens.

Chart for placement of Azalea pattern

Boston Fern
7-inch or 8-inch block
Ferns can be scattered among the wild flowers. Several shades and different green prints will give variety to the design. Clip edges as needed when turning under the seam allowance.

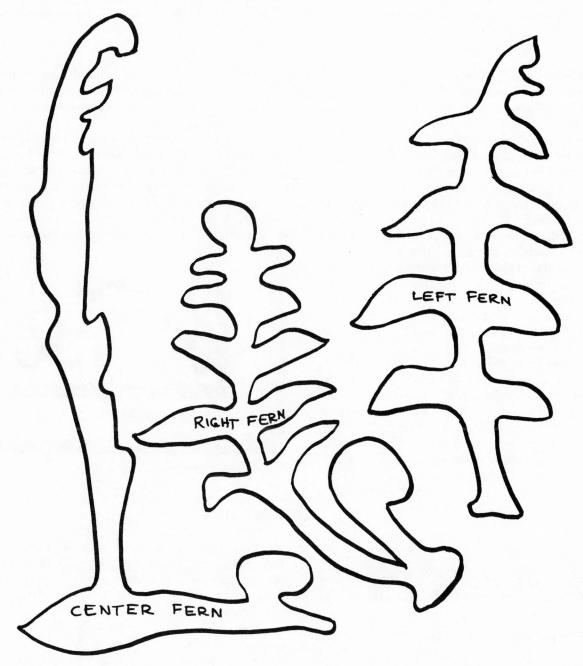

Boston Fern

THE IMPORTANCE OF BORDERS

Considering the Possibilities

After setting blocks together you will want to make an effective border. A narrow band is sometimes sufficient, but usually one or two narrow strips added to a wide strip in the dominant color make a good frame for the quilt. A painting is not complete without its frame. A border on a quilt serves the same function, preventing the eye from moving away from the center portion.

Dr. William Dunton, the physician who conducted a study of Baltimore-area antique quilts, maintained that a top wasn't worth doing if it was not completed with a compatible border. Your finishing stage must receive the same careful planning as the preceding stages. A border in perfect harmony with the interior is the final touch for any quilt.

Florence Peto, in her book *American Quilts and Coverlets,* suggests that you can't go wrong by adding a wide white, finely-quilted broadcloth border. For the less skilled quilter, a pattern or floral print border will do. She advises the maker to see that quilt-top corners and edges are true and even to assure a well-fitted border. Peto's book praises the pieced border, especially the Sawtooth with its light and dark triangles joined in a row. Two rows of Sawtooth separated by a solid strip produce even more handsome results. Chained Squares, Checkerboard Squares, and Wild Goose Chase are a few of the classic borders found on old American quilts.

Once you have become aware of borders, you will notice many unusual solutions to the finishing of quilts. Look at corners. Often you will see a vine pattern that wanders astray at a corner, because the maker did not know how to execute the turn. A thinking quilter would have analyzed the situation and made an appropriate movement of pattern.

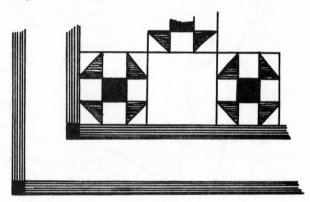

Triple border with corner squares

Amish quilters are fond of blocking corners with a contrasting-color square, often using one or more wide, elaborately quilted bands for borders. The same solution can be applied to pieced borders. A pieced block unlike the border piecing can be set at the corner to break the design, thus eliminating the problem of turning the corner.

Designing A Border

The border of a quilt should be in harmony with its central portion. If it supports and complements the rest of the quilt, it will be doing its job. If it is too weak or too powerful, the total composition will be unsuccessful.

A border should be well proportioned, but there is no formula. The width depends on several factors: amount needed to make the top large enough for the bed, intensity of the pattern, size of the blocks, color available for bordering, individual preference. When a top is ready to be

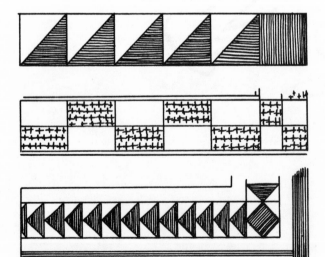

Borders: Sawtooth, Brick, Wild Goose Chase

Pieced border by Flavin Glover

finished, if a border plan has not been prepared, try the trial-and-error method.

Take several pieces of cloth that seem to have possibilities. Lay one against the edge of the top. Vary the width of the strip. Add another piece of fabric next to the first. Make as many combinations and variations as you can think of and choose the one that pleases you. You will know when you find the right one.

A border is sure to reflect and refine the center when it repeats one or two of the colors and even one of the motifs. The same colors, proportions,

Appliquéd border

and repetitions give movement of rhythm essential to any work of art, and you want your quilt to be considered art.

For an appliqué quilt, you may choose to settle on several bands of color rather than continue with appliqué on the border. If you wish to continue the appliqué, cut your design out of a piece of newspaper and lay it on the border strips to check your spacing. For safety's sake, be sure to allow a little extra material in length of strips when you cut your borders.

In *The Standard Book of Quilt Making*, Marguerite Ickis says, "The eye must follow the design easily as it makes its way clearly and in perfect balance. Ask a quilt connoisseur which part of the quilt receives her keenest attention, and she will surely tell you—the corners!" She cites an old superstition which says broken and stray ends at corners foretell disasters, so plan ahead.

Appliquéd border

If you are a quilt-slide collector, take shots of corners when you do close-ups. You will find some strange and wonderful corners that may have gone unnoticed when you were concentrating on over-all motifs.

Examine your own quilts and test the success of the borders. How do they rate? What could you have done to make them better? Plan, then make a few doll quilts to get a better understanding of the complete unity of border to quilt-block design.

The Rose of Sharon: *A Perfect Bride's Quilt*

The Rose of Sharon is an age-old flower. Its name derives from the lines that begin chapter two of the Bible's Song of Solomon: "I am the rose of Sharon, and the lily of the valleys." The song's lyrical quality is a delight after reading of Old Testament lineages and warring kings. In the years when books were scarce, young women turned to it for promises and dreams.

I have a copy of the will executed by my great-great-great-grandfather, Jacob Miller, Sr., of Jonesborough, Tennessee, in 1857. He left to his granddaughter, Mary Devault, certain furniture and furnishings, a black Durham heifer, and also "my quilted quilt of the pattern known and called the Rose of Sharon." What became of the quilt I do not know.

This popular pre-Civil-War pattern was a dress-up quilt to save for special occasions; thus, many fine examples still exist in numerous varieties. New cloth was purchased for these quilts and colors chosen with care. The best quilting went into a Rose quilt, as it was intended to be one's finest quilt. The illustrated block is part of a well-preserved quilt belonging to Mike and Linda Williams. It was made and quilted with unusual beauty by Mike's great-grandmother Jackson of New Salem, Tennessee, about 1850.

Her design is well suited to a fourteen-inch block. Make nine blocks; place them on the diagonal with alternating plain blocks. Add one or more borders, perhaps appliquéing a budded vine on the outermost. You may want to repeat the appliqué motif or choose another quilting design for the plain blocks. Whatever the choice, the finished quilt will be one of your best efforts.

ROSE OF SHARON
Maker: Mrs. Jackson
New Salem, Tennessee, 1848
Red, rose, and green cotton fabric on white.

CORNER
BUD
CUT 4

CUT 1

CUT 1

CUT 1

CUT 4
GREEN

CUT 1

CUT 4
GREEN

SIDE
BUD
CUT 4

Rose of Sharon
14-inch block
The block is suitable for a center medallion, wall hanging, or
pillow, as well as for a "best" quilt.

Turkey Tracks: *A Quilt for a Small Bed*

When Virginia McRae called to say she had an old Turkey Tracks quilt to show me, I expected to see the familiar blue three-pointed, curved tulip-like shape, sometimes called *Wandering Foot.* "Sleep under a Wandering Foot quilt and you'll always be a rovin'," an old saying goes.

I was surprised, then, to see Virginia's quilt was a version of another popular old pattern, North Carolina Lily, arranged in a color sequence so it resembled turkey tracks. I do not know the origin of the design or whether other quilters have made the same interpretation, but I rejoice in the lively quilt that came from so simple a pattern. What a treat to find a familiar quilt design used in a new way!

Elizabeth Ann Roberts Stegall of Kingston, Tennessee, Mrs. McRae's great-great-grand-mother, had embroidered "MSS" on the quilt for her grandson, Michael Sellers Stegall. Michael and his wife, Mifflin, saved their quilt for special occasions and handled it carefully. Eventually the Turkey Tracks quilt went to Michael's niece, Annie Elizabeth Stegall Blair and then to Virginia Blair McRae.

Injured by a goat and crippled, the quilt's maker had spent much of her life on a pallet cutting and joining small bits of cloth to make a finished quilt top—both a challenge and a reward. She supplied her children and grand-children with fine examples of her work.

The blocks for this Turkey Tracks were done on a scale small enough to approximate the actual size of a turkey's foot. Bright solid red and red-and-pink calico combine with tan (probably a faded green) and white to make a 3-inch square. Five of these units are set together with alternate white squares to make a Nine Patch. The pieced 9-inch block then alternates with 9-inch squares of solid white. The turkey tracks are set in the same direction throughout, with the red square standing out to give a delightful rhythm to the pattern. The resulting quilt looks like a flock of turkeys has marched across the bed. Try this one for a crib or small bed.

TURKEY TRACKS
   Maker: Elizabeth Ann Roberts Stegall
   Roane County, Tennessee, 1870
   Pieced blocks of solid red, red-and-pink calico, tan (probably faded from green), and white cotton fabric, alternating with white blocks.

Make the 3-inch tracks, set them together in a Nine Patch; then join alternately with 9-inch white blocks. The plain block provides a place for some fancy quilting. One or two narrow borders will set off the pattern of the piecing and frame your work. Be sure to work in your initials, the date, and initials for whom the quilt was made, just the way Elizabeth Ann did long ago.

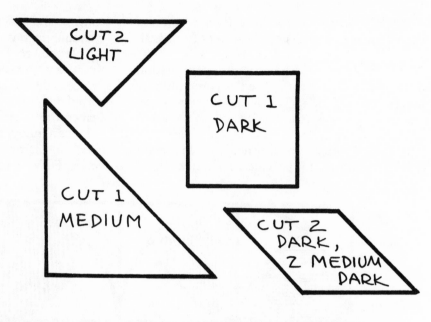

Turkey Tracks
9-inch or 12-inch block
Two patterns are given. The 3-inch units in the upper section, when joined with 3-inch plain squares (plus seam allowance), make 9-inch blocks. The larger pattern makes a 12-inch block. Join with 4-inch (plus seam allowance) squares. A North Carolina Lily design can be made by combining pieced units with plain squares and adding appliquéd leaves.

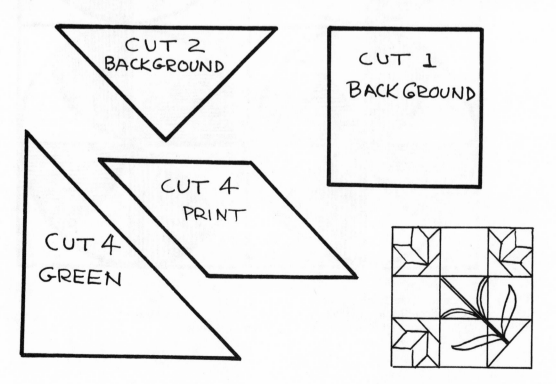

TVA Turbines: *A Show of Power*

In 1982, Judy Elwood, Alice Richardson and Joyce Tennery, three avid quiltmakers from Oak Ridge, Tennessee, published *Tennessee Quilting: Designs Plus Patterns*. The book is a compilation of the authors' patterns as well as some old and new patterns of the region. Many visitors to the Knoxville World's Fair considered the book a welcome souvenir.

In 1933 Congress established the Tennessee Valley Authority to provide electricity, flood control and navigable waterways for an area affecting the seven southern states through which the Tennessee River runs: Alabama, Georgia, Kentucky, Mississippi, North Carolina, Tennessee, and Virginia. In 1936 Norris Dam was completed—the first of 54 TV dams that reshaped the South.

Joyce Tennery's TVA Turbines quilt marks that epoch in history and reminds us of the importance of TVA's influence on our area.

TVA TURBINES
Designer: Joyce Tennery
Oak Ridge, Tennessee, 1982
Quilt patterns reflect present-day themes as well as those of the past.

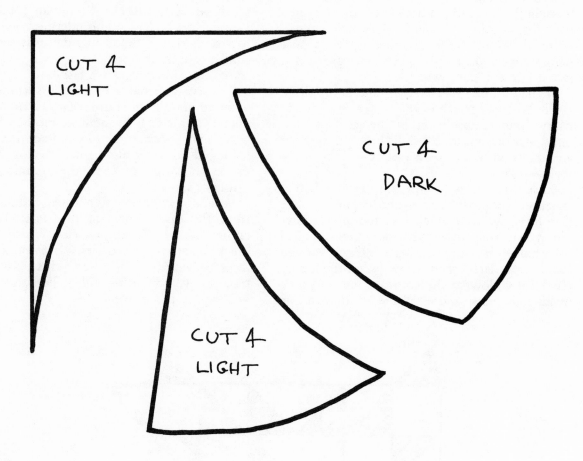

TVA Turbines
The pattern is for one square. It takes four squares to make
the 14-inch block.

Taylor's Victory: *Falling Star*

I have a special feeling about going to Jonesborough in east Tennessee, the first planned town in the state. My father's ancestors migrated there from Pennsylvania in 1790. I can find graves of relatives and those of other people whose names appear on family deeds and contracts. I feel at home in the town.

We had a fine Quilt Day in Jonesborough on April 20, 1985. Much of the success was due to Mary Granger, president of the local quilters' guild; her organizational skills brought together area quilts with the widest variety of designs and styles—many new to us.

Since this area was settled in the days before statehood by many residents of Virginia and the Carolinas, we were able to see old quilts representing a broad southern tradition. One quilt had been hidden in a cave during the Civil War and found years later; there were quilts stitched by Civil War widows, an Indian woman, young girls making dowries, and even a woman with one arm. Two types of quilts were especially memorable. One, Rocky Mountain Road of Scotland, a variation of the Rocky Mountain (New York Beauty) quilt, had a meandering vine in the Sawtooth strips. Before the day was over, two similar quilts appeared, but each quilter had traced the vine in her own fashion.

The second trio of unusual quilts seemed to be unnoted in quilt literature. Mary Granger found one; a later visitor brought in another, labeling hers Taylor's Victory. A third quilt of that pattern belonged to a family named Taylor, but the owner knew nothing about the circumstances of origin or name.

Several Taylors in Tennessee politics came from the eastern part of the state. Tall tales embellish some Taylor histories. Which one was the quilt pattern named for? Was it a political or a military victory? Do other quilts exist in this pattern? We hope time and quilters' enthusiasm will supply the answers.

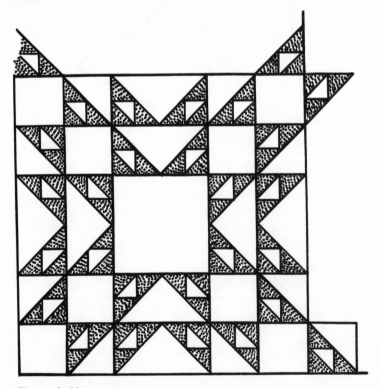

TAYLOR'S VICTORY
Maker: Martha Ellen Vaughn Taylor
Washington County, Tennessee, c. 1900
Red, brown, and blue assorted scraps with white, alternating with white squares.

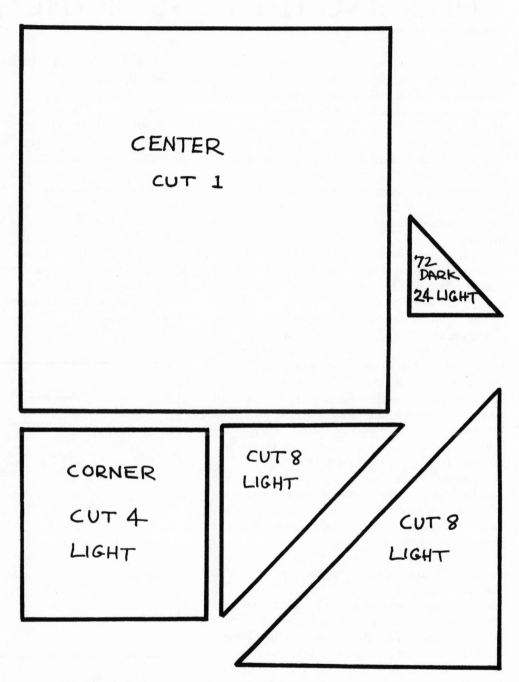

CENTER

CUT 1

72
DARK
24 LIGHT

CORNER

CUT 4
LIGHT

CUT 8
LIGHT

CUT 8
LIGHT

Taylor's Victory
12-inch block
Illustration shows continuation of pattern on adjoining
pieced blocks, alternating with plain block.

FINISHING THE EDGE OF THE QUILT

When a quilt has been completed and taken out of the quilting frame or hoop, it is an occasion for celebration. But a letdown may come with the realization that the edge has yet to be finished. Many people find the task of finishing the quilt a burdensome one.

The edge is an important part of your quilt's appearance and calls for the same consideration and planning as other stages of quiltmaking. A careless job of finishing may ruin a quilt's appearance no matter how fine the piecing and quilting.

Quilt edges can be finished in several ways. What works for one quilt may not be suited for another. You will have to determine what is best in each instance.

The simplest finish is the turned-over edge. There are two choices: turn the front edge to the back of the quilt, or turn the back edge to the front, and hem in place. If one of these methods seems appropriate, trim off the excess batting, check for squared-up corners, trim to make an even turning edge, and pin in place. Hem with a blind-stitch, not too widely spaced. Then finish with a row of quilting one-fourth inch to one inch inward, away from the hemmed edge.

A second method involves trimming the top and back edges, then turning them in so they come together to make a seam at the edge. This is called a knife edge. Join with a slip-stitch and finish with a row of quilting.

You may feel that a binding is the proper way to finish the quilt, and, for the most part, it is the preferred way to set off your best work. It gives a bit more of a frame than the other methods described. A binding that matches the border adds a smart look, while a contrasting border emphasizes the edge. A straight edge on the quilt does not have to be bound with a bias strip. The binding can be cut on the straight-of-the-goods, as were nearly all nineteenth-century quilt bindings. If you have curves or points to bind, you will need to use a bias strip. Bias tape wider than regular tape is available but it is not hard to cut your own edging, and you can use fabric that will have a longer-lasting quality. The curved edges of the Double Wedding Ring, for example, make a gently-curving scalloped edge best bound with a bias strip. The bias has "give" to it which enables the sewer to stretch or ease it around those scalloped edges.

How to Cut Bias Stripping

Choose a color and fabric in harmony with other fabrics used in the top. Wash and iron about one yard of material. Lay the cloth on a table, pick up the corner of one selvage edge, and bring it across the material until it is even with the cross-grain. The fold line will be at a forty-five-degree angle with the two straight edges; the fold line will be the true bias and the cutting line for the strips. Draw additional lines every 2½ inches (or the desired width) from the fold line. Cut with sharp scissors. Remove the selvages, match the ends, and join to make a continuous strip. Press seams open.

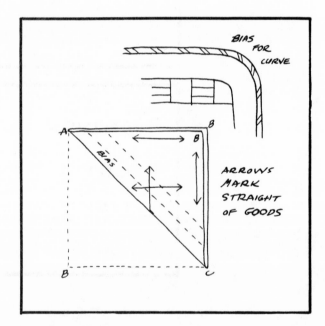

How to cut a bias strip

The suggested width makes a double fold of material for the binding. Place the two cut edges together, right side out, and seam to the top edge of the quilt. Then turn the binding over the edge and blind-stitch the folded edge to the back of the quilt. The double fold gives extra thickness so the binding will have a longer life than a single layer. In years to come, the binding can even be removed and turned to the good side when it becomes worn.

How to Cut Continuous-Strip Binding

You may want to try the continuous-strip method of making bias binding.

1. Take about a square yard of material; fold it diagonally and cut on the fold line, as shown.
2. Place the selvages and right sides together. Stitch the straight edge. Trim selvages. Press open.
3. On wrong side mark desired width with yardstick, measuring from cut edge.
4. Join ends together (straight-of-goods) *but offset by one row.* Cut on drawn line to make a continuous strip of bias. A thirty-six inch square will make a strip 2½ inches by thirteen yards.

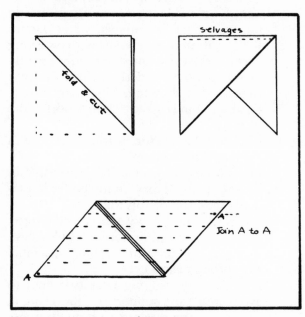

How to cut a continuous bias strip

The Last Steps

So many modern quilts seem to lack quilting near the outer edge. I have often been tempted to suggest the addition of a row or two of stitching next to the binding or even on it if the binding is wide. The extra quilting "sets" the quilt and gives it the completed look. Study edges at the next quilt show you attend and see if you agree with the way quilters have finished their work.

There are two more things to do before you are finished. Sign, date, and name your quilt in a pleasing way. Embroidery can be used in outline, back-stitch, or cross-stitch, either directly onto the quilt or on a separate piece of cloth sewn on later. While the signature is sometimes worked into the quilting, it is more difficult to read than embroidery unless the back-stitch is used for the quilting.

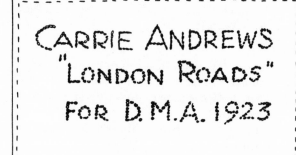

Embroidered quilt label

For those who don't like to embroider, the signature label can be typed on a piece of cloth, or written with permanent marking pen on cloth, and sewn to the back of the quilt. It is advisable to remove such labels when laundering the quilt.

Finally, photograph your quilt so you will have a record of it in case of loss, fire, or theft.

CARE AND PRESERVATION OF OLD AND NEW QUILTS

❖

Do
1. Use quilts. Sparing use of old ones will allow creases to rest.
2. Air quilts occasionally.
3. Wash, if in good condition. (See below.)
4. When storing, wrap in an old undyed sheet or towel.
5. Pre-wash all material to remove sizing before making a quilt.
6. Purchase acid-free boxes if that is your preferred storage method. (Suppliers include Light Impressions of Rochester, New York, University Products in Holyoke, Massachusetts or Talas Company of New York City.)

Don't
1. Put quilts away for a long period of time.
2. Fold the same way each time.
3. Store in tissue paper, unless it is special acid-free paper.
4. Store in plastic bags which gather moisture. Quilts need air.
5. Store in ordinary cardboard boxes.

Washing Quilts at Home
Washing quilts is a matter for careful consideration. An old and perhaps valuable quilt can be destroyed in laundering. When in doubt, seek advice. Before washing a quilt, examine it in the following way.
1. Place quilt on a flat surface. Cover a portion with a small plastic screen, edges bound in tape, and vacuum gently with handtool, to remove dust. Repeat over entire surface and on reverse side.
2. Test fabric before proceeding with wet-cleaning.
3. Determine fiber content. If in doubt, test a couple of threads of fabric if they can be obtained. Burn fiber to test. *Cotton* burns rapidly and smells like paper. *Wool* burns slowly and smells like burning hair. *Polyester* and *rayon* melt.
4. Determine the fiber content of the *filler*.
5. Test fabric for color-fastness. Put a few drops of the washing solution on each fabric and blot with blotter to test for fading. If fabric or fabrics are not fast, washing is not advised.
6. Cotton should be washed, not dry cleaned, since cellulose in dry cleaning fluid does not permeate the cotton fibers.
7. Don't wash cotton chintz. It may lose its glaze.
8. In mixed blends like wool/cotton or wool/silk, dry cleaning may be considered.
9. If a quilt is fairly new and in good condition, it may be washed in the washing machine on gentle cycle. An older quilt may be washed in the bathtub, but do not lift quilt in water or run water directly on quilt. Soak in softened water. Drain. Repeat if needed. Wash with washing agent. Agitate by squeezing sponge gently in water. Drain and rinse three to seven times. After draining, blot with towels. Finally roll in large towels to absorb more of water.
10. Use soft water for washing or add a softener (ex.: Calgon).
11. Use a mild detergent such as Orvus, Vali, Ensure, Joy or Ivory. Some prefer homemade lye soap, dissolved.
12. For bleaching, Snowy Bleach and Clorox II are acceptable, but not liquid bleaches.
13. Rinse thoroughly. In washing machine, run through extra cycle.
14. Dry quilt by hanging over two lines to avoid crease and support weight. Hang in shade or lay on mattress pads on the grass. Turn the quilt as it dries. In dryer, use *Air*, not *Heat* cycle.
15. Spot removal may be tried with:

    a. Lemon juice
    b. Efferdent denture cleaning solution and a cotton swab
    c. ¾ cup buttermilk, ¼ cup water, 2 tablespoons lemon juice (This chemical content is similar to the powdered bleaches mentioned above.)
    d. 1 ounce hydrogen peroxide, ¼ ounce sodium perborate, 1 quart distilled water

Do not fret over spots. Keeping the quilt in a neutral state, free from acid, dust, grit, sun, heat, cold, and moisture is the goal.

When Not to Wash Quilts

When a quilt is not color-fast, too fragile, glazed, or other, proceed in the following way.
1. Air outside over two lines to freshen and rest creases.
2. Vacuum lightly and gently on both sides through screen as previously described.
3. Use air cycle of dryer, but cautiously. Old fabric may split.
4. Use quilt some, but give it rest periods.

Preserving and Restoring Quilts

1. Avoid humid storage area.
2. Avoid excessive heat or cold for storage.
3. Shield fabric from sun and light-rays which destroy fibers.
4. If a few places in quilt need repair, proceed with caution. It may be possible to do minor mending with matching or similar fabric. Do not try to restore to a *new* condition. If you are searching for such material, here are some sources:
   a. Rummage shops may provide a used fabric to match that used in quilt.
   b. Buy an unattractive old top to use for mending.
   c. Mend crazy quilts with old silk ties, silk or cotton velvet.
   d. If necessary, bleach or dye reproduction prints to appropriate tone. If you use bleach, rinse *exceedingly* well.
   e. Dye colors needed.
   f. Sometimes tea or coffee dyeing is used, but it may cause fibers to rot.
5. It is often more desirable to hold a worn area together than to mend it. Sew silk organza or bridal illusion loosely over worn places. Ravelings of the silk may be used for thread; choose a #12 needle.
6. Organza or sheer net may be placed over a whole quilt if it is extremely worn and you wish to preserve it.
7. If a quilt is beyond use:
   a. Photograph it to save for remembrance, historical record, and research.
   b. Consult a knowledgeable person before discarding or cutting.
   c. If there are a few good portions, give a quarter to a quilt historian; frame a square or place a piece under a glass table top.
   d. Use any other ideas that will help you preserve some part in a tasteful way. (Clothing and toys not recommended!)
8. Sign, date, and put pattern name on all new quilts to preserve a record for the future.
9. Discover all the information possible about your old quilts. Using a marking pen or typewriter on a piece of cloth, label your quilt putting down all the facts you know: maker, date, place, pattern, owners, place purchased if applicable, date of mending, washing. Baste label to back of quilt. Remove for washing.
10. Keep documentation of your quilts, photos, measurements, description of pattern and materials, name of maker, date made, and all other information. File in a safe place.
11. If you have quilts you value highly, consider having them appraised and plan for their eventual dispersal.

For further information write:
Bets Ramsey
P. O. Box 4146
Chattanooga, TN 37405

BIBLIOGRAPHY

Beyer, Jinny. *The Scrap Look*. McLean, Virginia: EPM Publications, Inc., 1985.

Bonesteel, Georgia. *Lap Quilting with Georgia Bonesteel*. Birmingham: Oxmoor House, Inc., 1982.

Brackman, Barbara. *An Encyclopedia of Pieced Quilt Patterns*, Lawrence, Kansas: Prairie Flower, 1984.

Carter, Myra Adelaide Inman. *Diary, 1860–1865*, typescript. Chattanooga-Hamilton County Bicentennial Library, Chattanooga, Tennessee.

Elwood, Judy, Joyce Tennery, and Alice Richardson. *Tennessee Quilting: Designs Plus Patterns*. Oak Ridge: privately printed, 1982.

Fanning, Robbie and Tony. *The Complete Book of Machine Quilting*. Radnor, Pennsylvania: Chilton Book Co., 1980.

Finley, Ruth E. *Old Patchwork Quilts and the Women Who Made Them*, 1929. Reprint. Newton Center, Massachusetts: Charles T. Branford Co., 1970.

Gutcheon, Beth. *The Perfect Patchwork Primer*. New York: David McKay Co., Inc., 1973.

Hall, Carrie A., and Rose G. Kretsinger. *The Romance of the Patchwork Quilt in America*. New York: Bonanza Books, 1935.

Hassel, Carla J. *Super Quilter II*. Des Moines, Iowa: Wallace-Homestead Book Co., 1982.

Holstein, Jonathan. *The Pieced Quilt: An American Design Tradition*. Greenwich, Connecticut: New York Graphic Society, Ltd., 1973.

Hopkins, Mary Ellen. *The It's Okay If You Sit On My Quilt Book*. Atlanta, Georgia: Yours Truly, Inc., 1982.

Ickis, Marguerite. *The Standard Book of Quilt Making and Collecting*, 1949. Reprint. New York: Dover Publications, Inc., 1959.

James, Michael. *The Quiltmaker's Handbook*. Englewood Cliffs, New Jersey: Prentice-Hall, Inc., 1978.

The Second Quiltmaker's Handbook. Englewood Cliffs, New Jersey: Prentice-Hall, Inc. 1981.

Kentucky Quilt Project. *Kentucky Quilts 1800–1900*. Louisville, Kentucky: The Kentucky Quilt Project, Inc., 1982.

McKim, Ruby S. *101 Patchwork Patterns*. 2nd. ed. New York: Dover Publications, Inc., 1962.

Martin, Judy. *Patchworkbook*. New York: Charles Scribner's Sons, 1983.

Overstreet, Leslie W. *Speed Quilts*. Irvine, California: The Pisces Printer, 1979.

Peto, Florence. *American Quilts and Coverlets*. New York: Chanticleer Press, Inc., 1949.

Ramsey, Bets, and Merikay Waldvogel. *The Quilts of Tennessee: Images of Domestic Life Prior to 1930*. Nashville, Tennessee: Rutledge Hill Press, 1986.

Robertson, James I., editor. *The Diary of Dolly Lunt Burge*. Athens, Georgia: University of Georgia Press, 1962.

INDEX

Boldface indicates pattern with pieces.